Dan Clark's

Humor

File

A Repository of Jokes and B.S. Tales

Written or Compiled by

Dan Clark, CSP, CPAE

Published by:

IZZARD INK
—— PUBLISHING ——

ACKNOWLEDGEMENTS

For K.C., Danny, Natalie, Nikola, Ganes, McCall, and Alexandrea for finding wisdom, comfort, laughter, and solace in my speeches, stories, anecdotes, and words. I love you and need you in my life forever. Thanks for always laughing at my jokes and crazy observations, even though you've heard them at least 4,236,127 and ½ times before!!

For my grandchildren Aubree, Emma, Cora, Jack, and Luka for allowing me the enjoyment that comes from making them laugh!

For my inspirational, psycho, 'drain-bamaged,' humorous, crazy NSA friends Robert Henry, Jeannie Robertson, Grady Jim Robinson, Bob Murphy, Bubba Bechtol, Steve Rizzo, Dale Irvin, Jason Hewlett and everyone else in the world who has taken the time to remind us:

The Funniest Things Happen When You Look for Laughs!

TABLE OF HILARITY

PREFACE

When the publishers were trying to find someone to write this book, they called up the best-looking guy they knew. He turned them down. So, they called up the most intelligent guy they knew. He turned them down too. So, they called up the humblest, sweetest, most sincere guy they knew. Hey, I couldn't turn them down three times in a row, so I said yes!

By profession, I am a full-time speaker. No, I did not say "motivational speaker." I don't want to be a motivational speaker. They quote shallow cliché's like, "We become what we think about." That's not true. If that were true, I would have been a woman by the time I was twelve years old! I want to be an "inspirational" speaker. And yes, inspiration includes humor.

The only time we can take life more seriously is when we take ourselves less seriously. A sense of humor makes our idiosyncrasies acceptable and our short falls and failings bearable, which allows us to admit that we are okay just the way we are. For example, when I was born, I was so ugly that the doctor slapped me and then went out in the hall and slapped my dad! And as I grew older my dad kept the photo that came with the wallet! When I was in Junior High, I was so skinny I had to jump around in the shower to get wet!

On a friendship note: my buddy Bubba Bechtol, president of Bubbas of America and headlining country comedian, is one of the funniest men on earth. His entire act reminds us to laugh at ourselves. He is five feet eleven inches tall and weighs 340 pounds. He usually walks out on stage wearing a skimpy T-shirt, exposing his navel (thinks he's Shania Twain!). His opening line is "Hey, I beat anorexia! I got it into permanent remission, and it ain't coming back!" Bubba then continues, "I haven't always been this big. My doctor put me on a dehydrated food diet for six months and one day I got caught in the rain! It was awful! I gained 104 pounds in five minutes!"

Another very large friend was having chest pains. I was concerned and took him to our doctor friend, who was working that night in the emergency room. Trying to explain his predicament, he told the doc, "I'm overweight because it's a medical problem."

The doctor replied, "No. The only medical problem you suffer from is that your body retains too much chocolate fudge cake!" "But," my friend insisted, "obesity runs in my family." With a grin and an honest sense of humor, our doctor friend replied, "No, no one runs in your family!"

It's better to shoot for the stars and miss, than to aim for a pile of manure and hit!

Dan Clark
AND ASSOCIATES

ALL-TIME CLASSICS

Who Is This

A young soldier was working in the army supply building when he answered a telephone call. "Inventory check," the deep voice demanded.

The soldier reported, "We have 1500 rifles, 10 tanks, and one fat-headed sergeant's Jeep."

The voice on the other end said, "What?"

The soldier repeated, "We have 1500 rifles, 10 tanks, and one fat-headed sergeant's Jeep."

Angrily, the voice asked, "Do you know who this is?"

The soldier replied, "No."

"This is the Sergeant!"

The soldier gasped, "Whoa. Do you know who this is?"

The Sergeant answered, "No."

The soldier yelled, "Good. Bye, bye, fat-head!"

General's Secret

A young Army General finally got a chance to meet a

famous older General who had never lost a battle. When the young General asked him what his secret was, the older General explained, "I always led my men into battle, marching at the front of the line wearing a bright red shirt."

Perplexed, the young General observed, "But didn't that make you a target?"

The older General answered, "Yes. But when I got shot, the red color of my blood meshed perfectly with the red color of my shirt, and my men never knew I had been shot. So, they kept fighting until we won the battle. You should try it."

The young General replied, "Thanks. I will. Lieutenant, will you please bring me my brown pants?"

Defending Your Honor

A man was sitting at a table in the bar. Suddenly, two huge men came in the door, walked up to him, and beat the ever-living tar out of him. Leaving him unconscious and in a pool of blood on the floor, the two men strutted out of the bar. As they left, they stopped the bartender and proudly said, "When he wakes up, tell him that was Karate from Korea and Judo from Japan!"

In a few minutes the guy came to, stood up, wiped himself off, finished his drink, and left.

Later that day the two men came back to the bar. While they were drinking and laughing about the guy they beat up earlier that day, the guy they beat up walked back into the bar, straight up to their table and knocked both of them out cold. As he left he told the bartender, "When they wake up, tell them that was a crowbar from Sears!"

The Devil

In the middle of a preacher's sermon, the back door of the church slams open, and in walks the devil. Church members climb out the windows, and the preacher slides out the back door. However, one good old boy stays seated on his bench. The devil walks up to him and says, "Apparently, you don't know who I am."

The old boy says, "You're Satan."

The devil says, "Apparently, you don't realize that with one gesture, I can have you cast to outer darkness."

The old boy says, "Yeah."

The devil says, "Apparently you don't realize that with one word of my voice, I can have you tormented for eternity!"

The old boy says, "Yeah."

The devil asks, "Then why aren't you afraid of me?"

The good old boy says, "Listen, I've been married to your

sister for forty-two years, and there is nothing you can do that would surprise or intimidate me!"

Heavenly Spelling Bee

A woman died and St. Peter greeted her at the Pearly Gates with one question: "If you can spell the word 'love' you can enter into heaven." She answered, "L, O, V, E" and was invited in. Curiously she inquired if he asked everybody this same question. He said he did, and felt inspired to have her take over this important job.

One by one, she asked each person to spell 'love' until she suddenly saw her husband waving his hands at the back of the line. She called him to the front and asked him why he was there? How had he died so suddenly?

Sheepishly, he confessed that instead of attending her funeral that morning, he had gone golfing with his buddies. And on his way home he got hit by a bus and was killed.

"So," he asked, "What do I have to do to get into this heavenly place?" His wife answered, "Spell Czechoslovakia!"

Quick Thinking

A man was given a promotion in his company. The

president called him in and said, "We are impressed with your leadership skills. We need you to move to Detroit."

The man soured, "I don't want to move to Detroit. The only things Detroit has are good hockey teams and ugly women."

The president was offended, "What do you mean? My wife is from Detroit."

The man quickly replied, "Oh yeah, which team does she play for?"

Don't Drink and Ride

Monday night we went to a bachelor party, my friends got drunk, I was the designated driver and they talked me into taking them horseback riding on our way home. There was only one horse and before the groom could settle in on its back, it started bucking out of control until he was thrown face first to the ground. With his foot caught in the stirrup, his body bouncing off the saddle, and about to go unconscious, luckily the Wal-Mart manager came outside and unplugged it!

Temperature

An arrogant businessman had been in the hospital for

days, bossing the nurses around like his employees, who decided they would not check on him again. So, the head nurse came to the rescue, walked in his room, and told him she needed an accurate temperature. When he grunted and opened his mouth, she told him to roll over. After she inserted the thermometer, she left and did not close the door. For 30 minutes, people walked by giggling at the man on his stomach.

Finally, the doctor arrived and asked, "What's going on here?"

Angrily, the man answered, "What's the matter, Doc? Haven't you ever seen someone having their temperature taken?"

"Yes, said the doctor. "But never with a carnation!"

The Cover-Up

Two neighbor ladies had been feuding for months. One day they finally reconciled their differences and rekindled their friendship. They hugged and retired to their respective homes. Thirty minutes later one of the women was looking out her patio window and discovered her dog with something white in its mouth. It was her neighbor's pet rabbit.

"Oh, no," she said to herself. "I've just glued our relationship back together and my dog kills her rabbit!" So, she quickly took it into her home, washed it, blow-dried its fur into a beautiful fluff, and then tiptoed into her neighbor's backyard and secretly placed the dead rabbit in its hutch and locked the door. She thought all was well until she heard a blood-curdling scream. When she ran outside to greet her neighbor, she asked what was wrong?

Her neighbor blurted, "Our rabbit died two weeks ago, we buried it in the garden, and now it's back in its cage! Hallelujah!"

Sweet Mom

My 96-year-old mother went in for her annual physical and the physician told her she needed more exercise. So, she joined a fitness club and signed up for an aerobics class for seniors. Sure enough, she bent over, twisted and turned, jumped up and down, and perspired for an hour. But, by the time she got her leotard on, the class was over!

107 Years Old

A 107-year-old man was interviewed on The Tonight Show. Jimmy Fallon said, "It says here in your bio that you've been married seven times." The intense, energetic little man excitedly answered, "Yep. I loved them all, just outlived 'em all."

Fallon continued, "It says here that your current wife is thirty-five years old. Aren't you afraid of a heart attack?" The old man perked up, smiled, and quickly replied, "Hey, if she goes, she goes!"

Brutal Honesty

A police officer pulled over an older couple and said, "Sir, you were speeding, and you are not wearing your seat belt."

The elderly man scoffed and replied, "No, I wasn't speeding. Prove it. And I just took the belt off to talk to you!"

Exasperated, the officer turned to the wife. "Ma'am, your husband was speeding, wasn't he, and he probably hasn't had his seat belt on all day."

"Officer," she replied. "After forty years of marriage, I've learned never to argue with my husband when he's been drinking!"

Idiots in the Park

One day I was sitting on a bench on a folded newspaper. A man strolled by and asked, "Excuse me, are you reading that?" A few minutes later the same thing happened again, but this time I was ready. I was still sitting on the paper when a different man came up to me and asked if I was reading it. I stood up, turned the page, sat back down, and answered, "Yes, but I'll be done in a minute!"

God Father's Lawyer

A Mafia Godfather hired a bookkeeper who is deaf, knowing that because he can't hear, he will never be asked to testify in court. One day he finds out his bookkeeper has cheated him out of 10 million dollars. When the Godfather goes to confront him, he takes along his lawyer who knows sign language. The Godfather tells the lawyer to ask him where the money is.

The lawyer, using sign language, asks the bookkeeper, "Where's the money?"

The bookkeeper signs back, "I don't know what you are talking about."

The lawyer tells the Godfather, "He says he doesn't know what you're talking about."

The Godfather pulls out a pistol, puts it to the bookkeeper's head and says, "Ask him again or I'll kill him!"

The lawyer signs to the bookkeeper, "He'll kill you if you don't tell him."

The bookkeeper trembles and signs, "The money is in a brown briefcase, buried behind the shed at my cousin Bruno's house."

The Godfather asks the lawyer, "What did he say?"

The lawyer replies, "He says you're a whimp, and don't have the guts to pull the trigger!"

Concussion

The quarterback playing for the Aggies got hit so hard he was knocked unconscious. The coaching staff ran onto the field to help him. As the player came to, blinked his eyes, and shook his head, the assistant coach held up three fingers in front of his face and asked, "How many fingers do you count?"

The head coach immediately interrupted, "Oh man, he doesn't know that!"

TV Absurdity

Have you seen the confusing television ad where they demonstrate how the laundry detergent takes out bloodstains? The way I see it, if you've got a T-shirt covered in blood, maybe laundry detergent isn't your biggest problem!

What The Doctor Said

A man was having chest pains, and his wife insisted on taking him to the doctor. The doctor examined him and sent him out of the office, telling him to send his wife in for a private consultation.

The doctor told the man's wife that if she didn't wake up early every morning, deliver his breakfast in bed, rub his back, and drive him to work, he will die.

The doctor continued, "You must then fix and deliver a fresh, hot lunch to him every day at work, and rub his feet and back again, or he will die."

The doctor then concluded, "And when you pick him up from work and drive him home, you need to have a wonderful dinner ready for him, rub his back again, and cater to his every need until you tuck him into bed. If you don't do these things, he will die."

They left the doctor's office and started driving home. Her husband asked, "You were in there a long time. What did the doctor say?"

His wife looked at him and solemnly answered, "You are going to die!"

Lambada

My sweet, conservative dad was the consummate teacher. One evening when we were enjoying watching a television show together, an advertisement came on showcasing the hottest current movie, "Dirty Dancing." As the star Patrick Swayze held his dance partner in a provocative position and gyrated in a pelvic grinding motion, my dad asked, "Do they really dance that way these days?"

I answered, "Yea. They call it the Lambada."

"Whoa!" my dad replied, "We used to neuter dogs for doing that to our leg!"

Credit Card

My wallet was stolen. I waited three months before I reported it. The police detective asked me why I had waited so long to report a stolen credit card. I said, "Because the guy who took it was spending less money than my wife!"

If You Didn't See Me

A married man left work early one Friday afternoon.

Instead of going home, however, he squandered the weekend (and his paycheck) partying with the boys. When he finally returned home on Sunday night, he ran into an angry wife who screamed, "How would you like it if you didn't see me for a couple of days?"

"That would suit me just fine!" her husband said.

Monday went by, and the man didn't see his wife. Tuesday and Wednesday went by with the same result. Come Thursday, the swelling had finally gone down enough in his face that he could begin to see out of his left eye again!

Mood Ring

I bought my wife one of those mood rings. When she is in a good mood, it turns blue. However, when she is in a bad mood, it leaves a red mark on my forehead!

Average

On average, an American man under 60 will have sex two to three times a week, whereas a Japanese man the same age will have sex only one or two times a year. This is very upsetting news to most of my friends, as they had no idea they were Japanese!

Housework Challenged

One day a housework-challenged husband decided to wash his sweatshirt. Seconds after he stepped into the laundry room, he shouted to his wife, "What setting do I use on the washing machine? "It depends," she replied, "What does it say on your shirt?" He yelled back, "The University of West Virginia!"

Married Life

Three girlfriends had lunch. One is engaged, one is a mistress, and one has been married for 30 years. They decided to amaze their men by greeting them at the door wearing nothing but a black bra, stiletto heels, and a black mask over their eyes. They agreed to meet in a few days to compare notes. Their reports were as follows:

With a smile on her face, the engaged friend said: "When my fiancé came to pick me up for our date, and I answered the door naked, wearing only a black bra, black stilettos, and a black mask, we never left my house and made love all night long."

With a smile on her face the Mistress said: "I was at my lover's office when he arrived, and when he opened the door and saw me wearing only a black bra, black heels and a black mask over my eyes, we proceeded to make passionate love for the rest of the day."

With a frown on her face the Married wife reported: When my husband came home and I greeted him wearing only a black bra, black stilettos and a black mask over my eyes he said, "What's for dinner, Zorro?"

Boxing

A young man decided he wanted to be a heavy weight-boxing champion. He found a trainer and wanted to start working out. However, his trainer told him he didn't need to do anything except think positive. His first fight night arrived, and he was excited.

Round one began, and he was beat up. He staggered back to his corner, sat on the stool, and asked his trainer, "How am I doing?"

The trainer replied, "You're doing great. Just keep thinking positive. The guy hasn't even hit you yet."

Round two began, and he was again beat up so badly he crawled back to his corners and again asked his trainer, "How am I doing?"

The trainer replied, "You're doing great. Just keep thinking positive. The guy hasn't even hit you yet."

To this, the boxer immediately responded, "OK, but could you keep an eye on the referee, cause somebody out there is beating the hell out of me!"

PhD

All of the information in the world does not make a person successful. It's like the guy who has three PhDs: one in philosophy, one in psychology, and one in sociology. He doesn't have a job, but at least he can explain why!

Deodorant

I recently bought a new deodorant stick. The instructions said, "Remove cap and push up bottom." I can barely walk but when I pass gas the room smells lovely!

Dreams

A wife told her husband that she had a dream about bracelets, necklaces and diamond rings, and asked him what he thought it meant. Her husband smiled and giggled, "Wait until your birthday!"

On her birthday, she opened up a beautifully wrapped box that had a book in it titled, 'How to Interpret Dreams."

On top of Old
  Smokey

  All covered
  with snow

  I lost
my best bird dog
By aiming too low.

HILARIOUS STORIES

Baby Exam

A woman and a baby were in the doctor's examining room waiting for the doctor to come in for the baby's first exam.

Finally, the doctor arrived, examined the baby, checked his weight, and being a little concerned, asked if the baby was breast-fed or bottle-fed.

"Breast-fed" she replied.

"Hmmm. I think I better check some things. Will you please strip down to your waist," the doctor asked.

She undressed and the doctor began his exam. He pinched and pressed, kneaded, and rubbed in a detailed examination, squeezing and pressing for a full five minutes. Motioning to her to get dressed, he said, "No wonder this baby is underweight. You don't have any breast milk!"

"I know," she said. "I'm his grandmother, but I'm certainly glad I came."

As A Child

Two old friends were long-time neighbors living way out in the country. One day, they decided to hitch up the horse and buggy and ride into town to see if they could find a little action. When they arrived there was nothing going on, so they walked the aisles of the grocery store.

One old boy said, "Looky here. This box says Ex Lax— Makes You Feel Younger. Want to try it?"

The other agreed, and they bought two boxes.

They boarded their buggy and headed back home. One said, "Let's try it," so they split a box. Fifteen minutes later, still riding on the bumpy, rutted road, the other asked, "Feelin' any younger yet?"

"No," he replied. So they split the other box. Fifteen minutes later, still bouncing and vibrating up and down as the buggy took them home, one asked, "Are you feelin' any younger yet?"

The other, with a pale, sheepish grin slowly answered, "No, but I think I just did a mighty childish thing!"

The Raffle

Young Johnny moved to Texas and bought a donkey from a farmer for $100.00. The farmer agreed to deliver the donkey the next day. The next day he drove up and said, 'Sorry, son, but I have some bad news, the donkey died.'

Johnny replied, 'Well, then just give me my money back."

The farmer said, "Can't do that. I spent it already."

Johnny said, "Ok, then, just bring me the dead donkey."

The farmer asked, "What ya gonna do with him?"

Johnny said, "I'm going to raffle him off."

The farmer said, "You can't raffle off a dead donkey!"'

Johnny said, "Sure I can, watch me. I just won't tell anybody he's dead."

A month later, the farmer met up with Johnny and asked, "What happened with that dead donkey?"

Johnny proudly explained, "I raffled him off by selling 500 tickets at two dollars a piece and made a profit of $998.00."

The farmer said, "Didn't anyone complain?"

Johnny smirked, "Just the guy who won. So, I gave him his two dollars back."

Bar Dog

A man goes to a bar with his dog. He goes up to the bar and asks for a drink. The bartender says, "You can't bring that dog in here!"

The guy, without missing a beat says, "This is my seeing-eye dog."

"Oh man," the bartender says, "I'm sorry, here, the first one's on me." The man takes his drink and goes to a table near the door.

Another guy walks in the bar with a Chihuahua. The first guy sees him, stops him and says, "You can't bring that dog in here unless you tell him it's a seeing-eye dog

The second man graciously thanks the first man and continues to the bar. He asks for a drink. The bartender says, "Hey, you can't bring that dog in here!"

The second man replies, "This is my seeing-eye dog."

The bartender says, "No, I don't think so. They do not have Chihuahuas as seeing-eye dogs."

The man pauses for a half-second and replies, "What? They gave me a Chihuahua?"

Unexpected Laughs

A married couple went to Utah for a ski holiday. It was a beautiful spring day with perfect snow conditions and perfect weather but long lines at the lifts. Halfway through the day the wife needed to use the washroom, but because the slopes were crowded and she wanted to make the most of the day, she kept skiing. Run after run she put it off until eventually she gave in and headed for the facilities.

Her overzealous husband pleaded, "Just one more trip

up. You can have your comfort break when we get to the top of the mountain." But at the top, they found the washroom facilities in the lodge were clogged and temporarily closed. As they skied to the bottom, she was unable to hold it any longer. The woman told her husband to stand guard while she went into the trees.

Suddenly, with her skis still on and her pants down, the woman lost her balance and came shooting out of the trees going backward. Picking up speed, she flew across the ski run, hit the ski lift tower, and broke her leg. Her husband pulled up her pants, flagged down the ski patrol, escorted them down the mountain, and took her to the hospital.

Sitting in the emergency room, trying to take her mind off the pain, she engaged another patient in conversation. "Why are you here?" she asked.

"Lady," he responded. "You wouldn't believe what happened today. I was skiing and riding up the ski lift, when a woman came shooting out of the trees going backwards with her drawers down around her ankles. She hit the tower and broke her leg. I started laughing so hard that I fell off the ski lift and broke my arm!"

On the Job

A businessman was driving in the country when he came upon a sheepherder on the side of the road. He stopped and asked, "If I can tell you how many sheep you have, can I have one?"

The sheepherder agreed, so the man pulled out his laptop, did some calculations, and proclaimed, "You have 1,455 sheep." The sheepherder agreed and the man went into the field, picked his animal, and put it in the back of his car.

Before he drove away, the sheepherder asked, "If I can tell you what you do for a living, can I have my animal back?" The man agreed.

"You are a consultant," the sheepherder said.

"Yes, I am. How could you tell?"

The sheepherder replied, "You told me something that I already know. Now, can I have my dog back?"

Holidays

A man in Phoenix calls his son in New York and says, "I'm sorry I have to ruin your day, but I have to tell you that your mother and I are divorcing—forty-five years of misery is enough."

"Pop, what are you talking about?" the son screams. "We can't stand the sight of each other any longer," his father screams.

"We're sick of each other, and I'm sick of talking about this, so you call your sister in Chicago and tell her." He hangs up. Frantic, the son calls his sister, who explodes on the phone. "Like heck they're getting divorced," she shouts. "I'll take care of this."

She calls Phoenix immediately and screams at her father, "You are not getting divorced. Don't do a single thing until I get there. I'm calling my brother back, and we'll both be there tomorrow. Until then, don't do a thing. Do you hear me?" She hangs up.

Dad hangs up the phone and turns to his wife. "Okay," he says, "They're coming for Thanksgiving and paying their own airfares. Now what do we tell them for Christmas?"

Prison

An old gentleman lived alone in New Jersey and wanted to plant his annual tomato garden. However, it was very difficult work, as the ground was hard. His only son, Vincent, who used to help him, was in prison. The old man wrote a letter to his son and described his predicament:

Dear Vincent,

I am feeling pretty sad because it looks like I won't be able to plant my tomato garden this year. I'm just getting too old to be digging up a garden plot. I know if you were here my troubles would be over. I know you would be happy to dig the plot for me like the old days, but I understand. Love, Papa

A few days later he received a letter from his son.

Dear Papa,

Don't dig up that garden. That's where the bodies are buried. Love, Vinnie

At 4 a.m. the next morning, FBI agents arrived and dug up the entire area without finding any bodies. They apologized to the old man and left. That same day, the old man received another letter from his son.

Dear Papa,

Go ahead and plant the tomatoes now. That's the best I could do under the circumstances. Love you, Vinnie

Jesus is Watching

A thief breaks into a home while the residents are away. As he is stealing valuables, he hears a voice: "Jesus is watching you." He freezes and then continues filling his bag. The voice again says: "Jesus is watching you." This time, he goes to investigate, discovers a talking parrot, and asks if it's the one speaking. The parrot replies, "Yes." The thief asks, "What's your name?" The parrot answers, "Noah." The thief says, "What kind of idiot names their parrot Noah?" The parrot replies, "The same idiot who named their Rottweiler Jesus!"

You shouldn't try
to teach a pig to sing.
It's a waste of your time
and it annoys the pig!

—*Mark Twain*

I HATE
THIS...

Do not let what you
cannot do interfere with
what you can do!

Dan Clark
AND ASSOCIATES

RELATIONSHIPS/
MARRIAGE

Mother-In-Law Love

A man and his wife took his mother-in-law to the Holy Land on vacation. While there, his mother-in-law dies. He takes her body to the funeral home, and the funeral director explains that he has two options.

"I can ship your mother-in-law's body back to the USA for $5000. Or, for only $150, we can have a wonderful memorial service here in Jerusalem. Take your time to think about it and let me know."

The husband says, "I don't need to think about it! I want you to ship her body to the States right now for $5000!

The funeral director asked why. The husband replied, "A man lived over here two thousand years ago, he died, and came back to life in three days, and I don't want to take that chance!"

I Love You Honey

A man escapes from prison where he's been for 20 years. He breaks into a house to look for money and a gun and finds a young couple in bed. He orders the husband out of bed and ties him to a chair. Then ties his wife to the bed, climbs on top of her, kisses her neck, and goes into the bathroom. While he's in there, the husband says, "He's very dangerous and hasn't seen a woman in years. I saw him kiss your neck. So, if he wants sex, don't resist, do what he asks. If you make him mad, he will kill us. Be strong honey. I love you."

His wife responds, "He wasn't kissing my neck. He was whispering in my ear that he was gay, thought you were cute, and wanted to know if we had some Vaseline. I told him it was in the bathroom. Be strong honey. I love you too!"

Maturing Marriage

My wife hasn't spoken to me in the last four days, and I don't have a clue what I did. Which is a shame because I'd like to do it again!

Sometimes it's hard for me when my wife can't remember where she left her phone, but she remembers what I said five years ago on Monday at 3:34 PM.

Aging Gracefully

I'm 60, and I'm rich! Silver in my hair, Gold in my teeth, Crystals in my kidneys, and an abundance of natural gas! Never thought I could accumulate such wealth!

Aging Worry

The real Russian Roulette is when you're 60 and you sneeze, not knowing whether you're going to throw your back out or poop your pants!

Spontaneous Love

Do you ever wake up, kiss the person sleeping beside you, and feel glad you are alive? I just did and apparently will not be allowed on this airline again!

Sobering Thought

British politician Bessie Braddock encountered an intoxicated Winston Churchill and tried to publicly humiliate him, saying, "Sir, you are drunk."

To which he replied, "And you, Bessie, are ugly. But I shall be sober in the morning, and you will still be ugly."

Arranged Marriage

I told my son, "You will marry who I choose." He said "no." I told him she is Bill Gates' daughter. He said, "Okay."

I called Bill Gates and said, "I want your daughter to marry my son. "He said "no." I told Bill Gates, "My son is the CEO of the World Bank." He said, "Okay."

I called the president of the World Bank and asked him to make my son the CEO. He said, "no." I told him my son is Bill Gates' son-in-law. He said, "Okay," and they lived happily ever after!

Wife Verses Husband

A couple drove down a country road for several miles, not saying a word. An earlier discussion had led to an argument and neither of them wanted to concede their position. As they passed a barnyard of mules, goats, and pigs, the husband asked sarcastically, "Relatives of yours?" "Yep," the wife replied, "in-laws!"

Mermaid Wishes

Three men were fishing when they met a mermaid who

offered each of them one wish. The first man said: "Double my I.Q." The mermaid waved her hand and surprisingly he started reciting Shakespeare.

The second man said: "Triple my I.Q." And suddenly he started doing math problems he didn't know existed.

The third man asked her to quadruple his I.Q. The mermaid asked, "Are you sure about this? It will change your whole life!" The man said, "Yes," so the mermaid turned him into a woman!

Husband Verses Wife

Steve and his buddies were hanging out and planning an upcoming fishing trip. Unfortunately, he had to tell them that he couldn't go this time because his wife wouldn't let him. After a lot of teasing and name-calling, Steve headed home frustrated.

The following week, when Steve's buddies arrived at the lake to set up camp, they were shocked to see Steve already sitting at the campground with a cold beer, fishing rod in hand, and a campfire glowing.

"How did you talk your wife into letting you go?" One buddy asked.

"I didn't have to," Steve replied. "Yesterday, when I went home and slumped down in my recliner with a beer to drown my sorrows because I couldn't go fishing, my wife snuck up behind me wearing a sexy negligee and whispered, "Carry me into the bedroom, tie me to the bed, and do whatever you want. So, Here I am!"

Breast Feeding

A man was riding a full bus, minding his own business, when the gorgeous woman next to him started to breastfeed her baby. The baby wouldn't take it so she said, "Come on sweetie, drink this or I'll have to give it to this nice man next to us. Five minutes later the baby was still not feeding, so she said, "Come on, honey. Take it or I'll give it to this nice man here."

A few minutes later the anxious man blurted out, "Come on kid. Make up your mind! I was supposed to get off four stops ago!"

Blanket

A man was riding a train and eating in the dining car. The maître interrupted him, "Excuse me, we don't have any more room. Do you mind if this woman joins you?"

"No," the man replies, and they share the meal together. Suddenly, the porter runs in. "There is an emergency on board. We will have to double-up the occupants."

The man asks, "You mean you want me to stay with this woman? I can't. I'm a married man!"

The porter explains that it's a must. The man reluctantly conforms and walks the woman to his room. He waits outside while she goes in, gets ready for bed, and climbs up into the top bunk. He walks in, gets ready for bed, and climbs into the bottom bunk. Before long, and in the dark, he hears her voice. "I'm in a negligee and it's cold. Will you please bring me a blanket?"

The man replies, "Do you want to pretend we are married, just for a minute?"

In a sultry voice she answered, "Yeah."

He said, "Good. Get your own blanket!"

When It's Time

A woman sits down at the bar and orders a drink. She chugs it, pulls something out of her handbag, looks at it, puts it back, orders another drink, chugs it, pulls out the same something from her bag, looks at it, puts it back, and orders another drink. After her sixth drink the bartender finally asked what she kept looking at. The woman stood to leave and replied, "After each drink I look at a photo of my husband. When he finally gets good looking, I know it's time to go home!"

Think About It

A couple was having a tough time getting pregnant when an old timer told them that the secret to long life and fertility is to sprinkle a little gunpowder on your breakfast cereal every morning and all would be well. Sure enough, as he grew older and finally died at 95 years old, he left 12 children, 24 grandchildren, 30 great-grandchildren, and a 17-foot hole in the wall of the crematorium!

Internet Explanation of Where Babies Come From

A little boy goes to his father and asks, 'Daddy, how was I born?" The father answers, "Well, son, I guess one day you will need to find out anyway! Your Mom and I first got together in a chat room on Yahoo. Then I set up a date via e-mail with your mom and we met at a cyber-cafe. We sneaked into a room and Googled each other. There, your mother agreed to a download from my hard drive. As soon as I was ready to upload, we discovered that neither one of us had used a firewall, and since it was too late to hit the delete button, nine months later a little Pop-Up appeared that said: "You've got Male!"

Art Collector's Wife

A New York attorney representing a wealthy art collector called and asked to speak to his client, "Saul, I have some good news and, I have some bad news."

The art collector replied, "I've had an awful day; let's hear the good news first." The lawyer said, "Well, I met with your wife today, and she informed me that she invested $5,000 in two pictures that she thinks will bring a minimum of $15-20 million."

Saul replied enthusiastically, "Well done! My wife is a brilliant businesswoman. You've just made my day. Now I know I can handle the bad news. What is it?"

The lawyer replied, "The pictures are of you with your secretary."

Cowboy's Tombstone

It's important to have a woman who helps at home, cooks from time to time, cleans up and has a job to help pay the bills.

It's important to have a woman who can make you laugh.

It's important to have a woman you can trust, who never lies to you.

It's important to have a woman who is good in bed and loves to be with you.

And it's very, very important that these four women do not know each other or you could end up dead like me!

Big City

A young country hick came into the city for an MRI at the hospital. He had never been to a big city before and walked into the lobby of his hotel to check in. Not knowing what an elevator was or how it worked, he was startled when the lights flashed, the tone chimed, and the doors slid open. Before they could close, on walked a wrinkled, hunched-over, 80-year-old-woman with grey hair, wearing a frumpy faded dress. The doors then closed. 15 seconds later the lights again flashed, the tone chimed, the doors re-opened, and out walked a young, beautiful, blonde supermodel in a mini-skirt and heels. Scratching his head in disbelief, the country-bumkin whispered, "Shoulda brought my wife!"

He then proceeded to the clinic for his test. He was put into the MRI machine by an attractive, young technician. Sometime later, when the examination was over, and he was helped out of the machine by a much older woman, the young man again scratched his head, wondering, "How long was I in there for?"

Edjamakation

I remember greeting relatives at my high school graduation who were in shock because they all thought seventh grade was my senior year! No, I wasn't a great student and thank God my dad cut me some slack. Once I came home from school with a report card that had four F's and one D on it. My dad responded, "Son, looks to me like you're spending too much time on one subject!"

Yes, my cholesterol count was higher than my SAT scores, but I was never tempted to cheat because one time my buddy got caught. While taking a test, I overheard him whisper to his friend, "How close are you to the answer?" To which his friend replied, "About two seats away!"

Then the teacher yelled, "You are cheating!"

He rebutted, "No I'm not!" "Yes, you are." "No, I'm Not!" "Yes, you are!" "How do you know?" he finally broke down and asked.

The teacher replied, "The girl you are sitting next to wrote on her test paper, "Don't know the answer. You wrote, "Me neither!"

Gotta Love Grandmas

A doctor who had been seeing an 80-year-old woman for most of her life finally retired. At her next checkup, the new doctor told her to bring a list of all the medicines that had been prescribed for her. As the doctor was looking through these, his eyes grew wide as he realized Grandma had a prescription for birth control pills. "Mrs. Smith, do you realize these are birth control pills?"

"Yes, they help me sleep at night."

The doctor replied, "Mrs. Smith, I assure you there is absolutely nothing in these to help you sleep."

She smiled and patted the young doctor's knee, "Yes, dear, I know that. But every morning, I grind one up and mix it in a glass of orange juice that I give to my 16-year-old Granddaughter. Believe me, every morning she drinks it helps me sleep that night!"

Gay Marriage

If you are against gay marriage, the solution is simple! The next time a gay man proposes to you, just say, 'No Thank You.'

Bi?

If you are attracted to both men and women but neither of them is attracted to you, it means you are Bi-Yourself!

Marriage Advice

My wife and I were happy for twenty years. Then we met. Some people ask the secret of our long marriage. We take time to go to a restaurant two times a week. A little candlelight, dinner, soft music and dancing. She goes on Tuesdays, I go Fridays. The other night I had some words with my wife, and she had some paragraphs with me. I don't know about you, but I've had bad luck with both my wives. The first one left me, and the second one didn't. — Henny Youngman

Colors

A little boy asks his mom at a wedding, "Mommy, why is the girl dressed all in white?"

Mom answers, "She is in white because she is very happy and this is the best day of her life."

The boy nods and then says, "OK, and why is the boy all in black?"

A Housewife's Prayer

Dear Lord, I pray for wisdom to understand my man, love to forgive him, and patience for his moods.

Because Lord, if I pray for strength, I will beat him to death!

Marriages

I have an older aunt who had been married four times—first to a banker, then to an entertainer, a preacher, and finally a funeral director. When asked why she had married that many times and to such a diverse mix of men, she had a great reply, "One for the money, two for the show, three to get ready, and four to go!"

Difference Between Men and Women

Wife's Diary:

Tonight, my husband was acting weird. We had made plans to meet at a nice restaurant for dinner. I was shopping with my friends all day long, so I thought he was upset because I was late, but he made no comment on it.

The conversation wasn't flowing, so I suggested that we go somewhere quiet so we could talk. He agreed but didn't say much. I asked him what was wrong; He said, "Nothing." I asked him if it was my fault that he was upset. He said he wasn't upset, that it had nothing to do with me, and not to worry about it.

On the way home, I told him that I loved him. He smiled slightly and kept driving. I can't explain his behavior. I don't know why he didn't say, "I love you, too."

When we got home, he wanted nothing to do with me anymore. He just sat there quietly and watched TV. Finally, I decided to go to bed. About 15 minutes later, he came to bed. He fell asleep; I cried. I don't know what to do. Is he having an affair?

Husband's Diary:

A two-foot putt? It was a flipping two-foot putt! Who in the world misses a two-foot putt?!

The Confession

Hi Bob. This is Alan next door. I'm sorry buddy, but I have a confession to share with you. I've been riddled with guilt these past few months and have been trying to pluck up the courage to tell you to your face, but I am at least now telling you in text as I can't live with myself a moment longer without you knowing. The truth is I have been sharing your wife, day and night when you're not around. In fact, probably more than you. I haven't been getting it at home recently, but that's no excuse, I know. The temptation was just too much. I hope you will accept my sincerest apologies and forgive me. I promise that it won't happen again. Please come up with a fee for usage, and I'll pay you. My regards, Alan.

Bob's Reaction:

Bob, feeling insulted and betrayed, grabbed his gun, and shot his neighbor dead. He returned home where he poured himself a stiff drink and sat down on the sofa. He took out his phone, where he saw he had a new missed message from his neighbor:

Alan's Second Message:

Hi Bob. This is Alan next door again. Sorry about the slight typo on my last text. I expect you worked it out, but as I'm sure you noticed that my Autocorrect changed WIFI to 'Wife'. Crazy technology, eh? Hope you saw the funny side of that. My regards, Alan

Female Creation

God may have created man before woman, but there is always a rough draft before the masterpiece. Proof?

A man said to his wife one day, 'I don't know how you can be so stupid and so beautiful all at the same time. The wife responded, 'Allow me to explain. God made me beautiful so you would be attracted to me; God made me stupid so I would be attracted to you!

Help Me Officer

Husband: My wife is missing. She went shopping yesterday and has not come home.

Officer at Police Station: What is her height?

Husband: Gee, I'm not sure.

Officer: Weight?

Husband: Don't know. Not slim, not really fat.

Officer: Color of eyes?

Husband: Never really noticed.

Officer: Color of hair?

Husband: Changes a couple times a year.

Officer: What was she wearing?

Husband: Could have been pants, I don't know.

Officer: What kind of car did she go in?

Husband: She went in my Jeep.

Officer: What kind of Jeep was it?

Husband: It's a beautiful royal blue 2019 Rubicon with Sprintex Supercharger and Intercooler, Teraflex Falcon 3.3 Shocks, 1350 RE Reel Drive Shafts, Toyo Tires, Seward LED Light bar, Crusher Fenders, Wild Boar Grille, and a Tuffy Drawer. Totally custom and the envy of every friend!

At this point, the husband started choking up until the Officer interrupted to comfort him: "Don't worry, buddy. We'll find your Jeep!"

School Ride

A five-year-old girl was usually driven to school by her grandfather, but this morning she was taken by her grandma. That night she told her parents that the ride was very different than when grandpa took her. Her parents asked, "How so?" "Well," she said. "We didn't see a single numb nuts, blind bat, or freakin moron on the road the whole way!"

Motorcycle Man

A young girl was walking home from school when a man on a motorcycle pulled up next to her and asked if she wanted to hop on the back and go for a ride. The girl said, "No!" The man continued to follow her and asked her if he paid her $10 would she let him give her a ride. She said "No!" And walked faster to get away. The man followed her and said, "This is my last offer. If I pay you $20 and give you a bag of candy, will you let me give you a ride?" The girl stopped, turned around and yelled, "No Dad! You are the one who bought that lame Honda instead of a cool Harley – you ride it yourself!"

HOW THE FIGHT STARTED

I told my daughter there was a job opening for a police officer. She said, "Why would I be a cop?" I said, "You chase the same men the cops do!" And that's when the fight started...

Husband goes with his wife to her high school reunion. After meeting several of her friends and former classmates, her bored and yawning husband suggests they sit down. Suddenly, the band cranks up the music and one guy starts break dancing, moon walking, doing back flips, and the splits. Pointing at him his wife says, "50 years ago he proposed to me and I turned him down."

Husband says: "Looks like he's still celebrating!" And that's when the fight started...

A husband was hinting about what he wanted for their upcoming anniversary. He said, "I want something shiny that goes from 0 to 310 in about 3 seconds." She bought him a bathroom scale. And that's when the fight started...

A father buys a lie detector robot that slaps people when they lie. He decides to test it out at dinner one night. The father asks his son what he did that afternoon. The son says, "I did some homework." The robot slaps the son. The son says, "Ok, Ok, I was at a friend's house watching movies." Dad asks, "What movie did you watch?" Son says, "Toy Story." The robot slaps the son. Son says, "Ok, Ok, we were watching a dirty movie." Dad says, "What? At your age, I didn't even know what a dirty movie was." The robot slaps the father. Mom laughs and says, "Well, he certainly is your son." The robot slaps the mother. And that's when the fight started...

One year, I decided to buy my mother-in-law a cemetery plot as a Christmas gift. The next year, I didn't buy her a gift. When she asked me why, I replied, "Well, you still haven't used the gift I bought you last year!" And that's when the fight started...

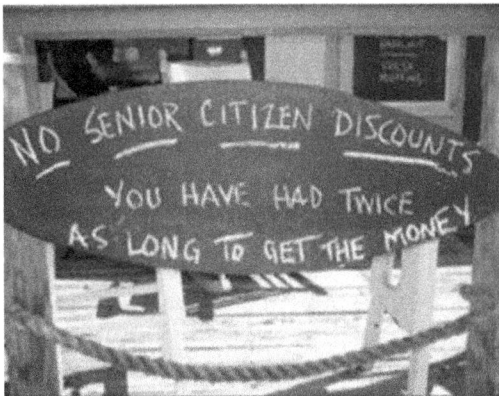

NO SENIOR CITIZEN DISCOUNTS
YOU HAVE HAD TWICE
AS LONG TO GET THE MONEY

SENIORS SAY/DO

THE DARNDEST THINGS

Grandma

When my grandmother was 61 years old, she started walking five miles every day. Now she is 91 and we don't know where she is!

Grandpa

I changed my car horn to gunshot sounds. People move out of the way much faster now!

Easter

When we get old, easter egg hunts are even more exciting! We can hide our own easter eggs, wait half an hour, and have no clue where we put them!

Surgeon

An elderly man was on the operating table awaiting surgery to be performed by his son, a renowned surgeon. Just before they would put him under, he asked to speak to his son: "Don't be nervous, son, do your best and just remember, if it doesn't go well, if something happens to me... your mother is going to come and live with you and your wife."

Talking Frog

An older man was walking in the woods when a frog jumped out of the grass and said, "Please, fine sir, if you will take me home and kiss me, I will turn into a beautiful princess and stay with you forever." The old man picked up the frog, put it in his pocket, and headed for home.

On his way, he stopped at the local store to show everyone his frog. Again, the frog repeated, "If you kiss me, I will turn into a beautiful princess."

The people couldn't believe it. "Quick—kiss it. Get your princess."

The old man paused, thought for a minute, and slowly replied, "Nah. At my age, I would rather have a talking frog!"

Under Oath

In a courtroom in Kentucky, an eighty-year-old man was called as a key witness for the prosecution in a murder trial. On the stand, the defense attorney tried to discount the validity of his testimony. He attacked the elderly man, "You mean to tell me that you saw the defendant shoot a man at ten at night?"

The old southern gentleman politely answered, "Yes, sir, I saw him do it with my own two eyes."

The defense attorney yelled, "You were fifty yards away! How far can you see in the dark?" The old man replied, "I can see the moon, how far's that?"

Don't Worry, Be Happy

One afternoon at a sales convention, an eighty-two-year-old man stepped up to the lectern. He spoke from the heart for a few minutes and then apologized for having to leave early. He said, "I've got to go. Tonight, my wife and I are celebrating our wedding anniversary. Yep. Me and my wife have enjoyed seventeen great years of marriage—seventeen out of fifty-five ain't bad!"

Counseling

After 35 years of marriage, a husband and wife came for counseling. When asked what the problem was, the wife went into a tirade listing every problem they had ever had in the years they had been married. On and on and on: neglect, lack of intimacy, emptiness, loneliness, feeling unloved and unlovable, an entire laundry list of unmet needs she had endured.

Finally, after allowing this for a sufficient length of time, the therapist got up, walked around the desk and after asking the wife to stand, he embraced and kissed her long and passionately as her husband watched - with a raised eyebrow.

The woman shut up and quietly sat down as though in a daze. The therapist turned to the husband and said, "This is what your wife needs at least 3 times a week. Can you do this?"

"Well, I can drop her off here on Mondays and Wednesdays, but on Fridays, I play golf."

Hard to Find

My friend told me he was thinking of divorcing his wife. I asked him why. He replied, "She hasn't spoken to me in two months." I told him to think twice about divorce – women like that are hard to find!

Fish Story

An elderly man was stopped by a game warden with two buckets of fish leaving a lake well known for its fishing. The game warden asked the man, "Do you have a license to catch those fish?"

Knowing he could be in big trouble the man replied, "No, sir. These are my pet fish."

"Pet fish?" the warden replied.

"Yes, sir. Every night I take these here fish down to the lake and let them swim around for a while. I whistle and they jump back into their buckets, and I take 'em home."

"That's a bunch of crap! Fish can't do that!" replied the warden in disbelief.

The man looked at the game warden for a moment and then said, "Here, I'll show you how it works," and the old man poured the fish into the lake.

After several minutes, the game warden turned to the man and said, "Well? When are you going to call them back?"

"Call who back?" the man asked.

"The FISH" the warden said sternly.

"What fish?" the man asked.

Senior Shades of Grey

After nearly 40 years of marriage, Charlie and his wife were lying in bed. Suddenly the wife felt Charlie begin to massage her in ways he hadn't done in quite some time.

It almost tickled as his fingers started at her neck and then began moving down past the small of her back. He then caressed her shoulders and neck, slowly worked his hand down, stopping just over her stomach. He then proceeded to place his hand on her left inner arm, working down her side, passing gently over her buttocks and down her leg to her calf. Then, he proceeded up her thigh, stopping just at the uppermost portion of her leg. He continued in the same manner on her right side.

But then he suddenly stopped, rolled over, and became silent. As she had become quite aroused by this caressing, his wife asked in a loving breathy voice, "Honey, that was wonderful. Thank you. Why did you stop?"

"He said, "I found the remote."

Stages Of Life

At age 4 success is: Not piddling in your pants.

At ages 1-9: You believe in Santa Claus.

At age 10-11: You don't believe in Santa Claus.

At age 12 success is: Having friends.

At age 16 success is: Having a driver's license.

At age 30: You are Santa Claus.

At age 35 success is: Having money.

At age 50 success is: Having money.

At age 60: You look like Santa Claus.

At age 70 success is: Having a driver's license.

At age 75 success is: Having friends.

At age 80 success is: Not piddling in your pants.

Senior Wedding

Jacob, age 92, and Rebecca, age 89, living in Miami, are all excited about their decision to get married. They go for a stroll to discuss the wedding, and on the way they pass a drugstore. Jacob suggests they go in.

Jacob addresses the man behind the counter:

"Are you the owner?" The pharmacist answers, "Yes."

Jacob: "We were about to get married. Do you sell heart medication and pills for circulation?"

Pharmacist: "All kinds."

Jacob: "How about suppositories and medicine for memory problems, arthritis, Alzheimer's and antidotes for Parkinson's disease?"

Pharmacist: "Absolutely."

Jacob: "You sell wheelchairs and walkers and canes and adult diapers?"

Pharmacist: "Yes, sir, we have everything you have asked for."

Jacob: "Wonderful! We would like to use this store as our Bridal Registry."

Tea

One day Grandma was out, and Grandpa was in charge of their three-year-old granddaughter, whose favorite toy was a little tea set. Grandpa was in the living room engrossed in the evening news when she brought him a little cup of tea, which was just water.

After several cups of tea and lots of praise for such yummy tea, Grandma came home. Grandpa made her wait in the living room to watch his precious little granddaughter bring him a cup of tea, gushing it was just the cutest thing!"

Grandma waited, and sure enough, here she came down the hall with a cup of tea for Grandpa. Both granddaughter and Grandma watched him chug the whole cup.

Then she said, (as only a grandma would know), "Did it ever occur to you that the only place she can reach to get water is the toilet?"

Lucky Night

An elderly man meets a hooker in a bar. She says, "It's your lucky night. I've got a special game for you. I will do absolutely anything you want for a hundred dollars, as long as you can say it in three words."

The good old boy pulls his wallet out of his pocket, lays a $100 bill on the bar and says, "Paint my house."

Getty Up

Lovely eighty-seven-year-old Rose was asked to speak at our college football banquet. She stepped up to the podium and began to shake so badly that she dropped her speech; 3x5 cards went everywhere.

In response, Rose leaned into the microphone and said, "Sorry. I'm so nervous. I gave up beer for Lent, and this whiskey is killing me!"

Then Rose taught us the lesson of the ages. She said,

"I've noticed how many of you college men are still wearing your old high school athletic letter jackets. Hey, I know you used to be a stud-muffin-hunk-of-burnin love, but when your horse dies, dismount!"

Dead Horse

Dakota tribal wisdom says that when you discover you are riding a dead horse, the best strategy is to dismount. However, in business, we often try other strategies with dead horses, such as:

- Buying a stronger whip

- Changing company riders saying: "this is the way we have always ridden this horse"

- Appointing a committee to study the horse

- Arranging to visit other sites to see how they ride dead horses

- Increasing the standards to ride dead horses

- Appointing a team to revive the dead horse

- Creating a training session to increase our riding ability

- Forming a quality circle to find uses for dead horses

- Promoting the dead horse to a supervisory position

Growing Old

I used to have a full head of thick blonde hair. Now I'm losing it on top and growing it in places I don't even need it - my nose and ears and back. My only hope is that the hair in my right ear grows long enough that I can comb it up over the top of my head and fake everybody out! And it's really scary when you start making the same noises as your coffeemaker. Then you bend over to pull up your socks and think, "What else can I accomplish while I'm way down here?" Then you go to bed perfectly healthy, and you wake up injured, and all you did was lie there!

Getting Older

An elderly gentleman was complaining about getting old. "I've had two bypass surgeries, a hip replacement, and new knees. I'm half blind, I can't hear anything quieter than a jet engine, I have hemorrhoids the size of golf balls, and I take forty different medications that make me dizzy, winded, and subject to blackouts. My right foot shakes, I have poor circulation and can hardly feel my hands and arms anymore. I can't remember if I'm eighty-five or ninety-two, and I have lost all my friends. But thank God, I still have my driver's license!"

Acting Old

They weren't in my pockets. Suddenly I realized I must have left them in the car. Frantically, I headed for the parking lot. My husband has scolded me many times for leaving my keys in the car's ignition. He is afraid that the car could be stolen.

As I looked around the parking lot, I realized he was right. The parking lot was empty. I immediately called the police. I gave them my location and confessed that I had left my keys in the car, and that it had been stolen. Then I made the most difficult call to my husband: "I left my keys in the car and it's been stolen."

There was a moment of silence. I thought the call had been disconnected, but then I heard his voice, "Are you kidding me?" He barked, "I dropped you off!"

Now it was my turn to be silent. Embarrassed, I said, "Well, come and get me."

He retorted, "I will, as soon as I convince this cop that I didn't steal your car!"

Being Old

A reporter was interviewing a 104-year-old woman. "And what do you think is the best thing about being 104?" the reporter asked. The woman simply replied, "No peer pressure."

You Know You're Getting Old If…

When you were a child, you thought nap time was a punishment. Now it's a mini vacation.

During breakfast, you hear snap, crackle, pop, but you're not eating cereal.

Your back goes out, but you stay home.

Your idea of weightlifting is standing up, and it takes two tries to get up from the couch.

Most of the names in your address book start with Dr.

You sit in a rocking chair and can't get it going.

It takes twice as long to look half as good.

You confuse having a clear conscience with a bad memory.

You finally get your head together, and your body starts falling apart. You wonder if you shouldn't have trusted that "toot!'

You don't feel old. You don't feel anything until noon. Then it's time to take a nap.

You've been trying to call your friend all day on your cell phone and suddenly realize it's your calculator!

"Getting Lucky" means walking into a room and remembering why you're there.

You don't need anger management. You need people to stop pissing you off. Your people skills are just fine - it's your tolerance of idiots that needs work.

You talk to yourself because sometimes you need expert advice!

Senior's Texting Vocabulary

BFF: Best Friend Fainted

BYOT: Bring Your Own Teeth

CBM: Covered by Medicare

FWB: Friend with Beta-blockers

LMDO: Laughing My Dentures Out

GGPBL: Gotta Go, Pacemaker Battery Low!

Normal

The interesting news is that in the 1960's, people took acid to make the world weird. The bad news is now that the world is weird, people are taking Prozac to make it normal.

Useful

Yesterday my son emailed me again, asking why I didn't do something useful with my time. Like sitting around the pool and drinking wine is not a good thing? I asked. Talking about me "doing- something-useful' seems to be his favorite topic of conversation.

He is "only thinking of me", he says and relentlessly suggests that I go down to the Senior Center and hang out with the gals. To patronize him I did it, but when I got home, I decided to play a prank on him.

I emailed him and told him that I had joined a Parachute Club. He replied, "Are you nuts? You are 78 years old and now you're going to start jumping out of airplanes?"

I told him that I even got a Membership Card and emailed a copy to him. He immediately telephoned me and yelled, "Good grief, Mom, where are your glasses?! This is a membership to a Prostitute Club, not a Parachute Club."

"Man, oh man, am I in big trouble," I said. "I signed up for five jumps a week and can't cancel my contract!"

Suddenly, the line went quiet until his friend picked up the phone and said my son had fainted.

Ha! Life as a Senior Citizen is not getting any easier, but sometimes it sure can be ever so much fun!

Swimming

Ron, an elderly man in Florida, had owned a farm for several years with a large pond in the back. It was properly shaped for swimming, so he fixed it up nice with picnic tables, horseshoe courts, and some orange and lime trees.

One evening the old farmer decided to go down to the pond, as he hadn't been there for a while, and look it over. He grabbed a five-gallon bucket to bring back some fruit. As he neared the pond, he heard voices shouting and laughing with glee.

As he came closer, he saw it was a bunch of young women skinny-dipping in his pond. So as not to appear to be a 'creeper,' he made the women aware of his presence, and they all went to the deep end.

One of the women shouted to him, "We're not coming out until you leave!"

Ron frowned, "I didn't come down here to watch you ladies swim naked or make you get out of the pond naked." Holding the bucket up, Ron said, "I'm here to feed the alligator!"

Irony

Going to bed early, not leaving the house, and not going

to a party – three of my major childhood punishments have now become my adult goals!

Four Bottles

Life can be summed up with four bottles: baby bottle, coke bottle, beer bottle, and intravenous feeding bottle.

Memory

A couple in their nineties are both having problems remembering things. They decide to go to the doctor for a checkup. The doctor tells them that they're physically okay, but they might want to start writing things down to help them remember.

Later that night while watching TV, the old man gets up from his chair. His wife asks, "Where are you going?"

"To the kitchen," he replies. "Will you get me a bowl of ice cream?"

"Sure."

"Don't you think you should write it down so you can remember it?" she asks.

"No, I can remember it."

"Well, I'd like some strawberries too. You'd better

write it down, because you know you'll forget it."

He says, "I can remember that!"

"I'd also like whipped cream. I'm certain you'll forget that, so you'd better write it down!" she retorts.

Irritated, he says, "I don't need to write it down! Leave me alone! Ice cream with strawberries and whipped cream. I got it, for goodness sake!"

After 20 minutes, the old man returns from the kitchen and hands his wife a plate of bacon and eggs. She stares at the plate and says, "Where's my toast?"

Retirement

I finally did some financial planning, and it looks like I can retire at 97and live comfortably for 11 minutes!

Old Geezer

An old physician, Doctor Gordon Geezer, became very bored in retirement and decided to re-open a medical clinic. He put a sign up outside that said: "Dr. Geezer's Clinic. Get your treatment for $500. If not cured, get back $1,000."

Doctor Digger Young, who was positive that this old 'geezer' didn't know beans about medicine, thought this would be a great opportunity to get an easy $1,000. So, he went to Dr.

Geezer's clinic and explained, "I have lost all taste in my mouth. Can you please help me?"

Dr. Geezer: "Nurse, please bring medicine from the box 22 and put 3 drops in Dr. Young's mouth."

Dr. Young: 'Aaagh! This is Gasoline!"

Dr. Geezer: "Congratulations! You've got your taste back. That will be $500."

Dr. Young gets annoyed and goes back after a couple of days figuring to recover his money stating: "I have lost my memory, I cannot remember anything."

Dr. Geezer: "Nurse, please bring medicine from box 22 and put 3 drops in the patient's mouth."

Dr. Young: "Oh, no you don't, that is Gasoline!"

Dr. Geezer: "Congratulations! You've got your memory back. That will be another $500."

Dr. Young, after having lost $1000, leaves angrily and comes back after several more days to declare: "My eyesight has become weak - I can hardly see anything!"

Dr. Geezer: "Well, I don't have any medicine for that so, "Here's your $1000 back" (giving him a $10 bill).

Dr. Young: "But this is only $10!"

Dr. Geezer: "Congratulations! You got your vision back! That will be another $500."

Moral of the story: Just because you're "Young" doesn't mean that you can outsmart an old 'Geezer!'

Old Age Questions and Answers

Q: What can a man do while his wife is going through menopause? A: Keep busy. If you're handy with tools, you can finish the basement. When you're done, you will have a place to live.

Q: Someone has told me that menopause is mentioned in the bible. Where? A: Matthew 14:92: "And Mary rode Joseph's ass all the way to Egypt."

Q: Why should 70-plus-year-old people use valet parking? A: Valets don't forget where they park your car.

Q: What is the most common remark made by 70-plus-year-olds when they enter antique stores? A: "Gosh, I remember these!"

Rose Colored Glasses

My face in the mirror isn't wrinkled or drawn
My house isn't dirty the cobwebs are gone
My garden looks lovely and so does my lawn
No, I'll never ever put glasses back on!

Conclusion

I think we can conclude that the "Time Out" generation did not work out as well as the "Ass Whoopin" generation!

Banks

A loan at a bank can take 30 years to pay off. But if you rob a bank, you're out in 10 years. Follow me for more financial advice!

EXERCISE AND SPORTS

The 'Good Ol Days'

Remember when you could refer to your knees as left and right instead of good and bad?

Getting Old

'Old' is not an age - it's when you stand in front of the mirror naked, and you see your rear end from the front without even turning around!

Perspective

I decided to change calling the washroom the "John" and renamed it the "Jim." I feel much better saying, "I went to the Jim this morning!"

I don't think anyone should run if no one is chasing them, and no weight should ever be lifted if it doesn't have to be moved!

I'm in shape. Round is a shape.

Rock and Roll

The fact that Keith Richards and Willie Nelson both outlived Richard Simmons has me rethinking this eating right and exercise thing!

Choices

In a span of 17 years, 114 people died in accidents while at the gym. In the same 17 years, only one man died while eating a donut. Life is about the choices you make!

Good Health

The good news is that I'm in pretty good health, which is the slowest possible rate at which one can die. The bad news is that we health nuts are going to feel awfully stupid someday, lying in the hospital, dying of nothing.

Health Club Saga

For my birthday this year, my wife Joan purchased me a

week of private sessions at the local health club. Though still in pretty good shape from when I was on the varsity chess team in high school, I decided it was a good idea to go ahead and try it. I called and made reservations with someone named Tanya, who said she is a 26-year-old aerobics instructor and athletic clothing model. My wife Joan seemed very pleased with how enthusiastic I was. They suggested I keep an "exercise diary" to chart my progress.

Day 1: Started the morning at 6:00 a.m. Tough to get up, but worth it when I arrived at the health club and Tanya was waiting for me. She's something of a goddess, with long muscular legs that went all the way to the floor, with curly blonde hair and a dazzling white smile. She showed me the machines and took my pulse after five minutes on the treadmill. She seemed a little alarmed that it was so high, but I think just standing next to her in that outfit of hers added about ten points. Enjoyed watching the Aerobics class. Tanya was very encouraging as I did my sit-ups, though my gut was already aching a little from holding it in the whole time I was talking to her. This is going to be great! I love this, and I think I love Tanya!

Day 2: Took a whole pot of coffee to get me out the door, but I made it. Tanya had me lie on my back and push this heavy iron bar up into the air. Then she put weights on it, for heaven's sake! Legs were a little wobbly on the treadmill, but I made it the full two minutes. Her smile made it all worthwhile. This is great and I think I love Tanya.

Day 3: The only way I can brush my teeth is by laying the toothbrush on the counter and moving my mouth back and forth over it. I am certain that I have developed a hernia in both pectorals. Driving was OK as long as I didn't try to steer. I parked on the sidewalk right in front of the door so I could crawl into the building. Thirty minutes into my workout Tanya was a little impatient with me and said my screaming was bothering the other club members. The treadmill hurt my chest, so I did the stair monster. Why would anyone invent a machine to simulate an activity rendered obsolete by the invention of elevators? Tanya told me regular exercise would make me live longer. I can't imagine anything worse.

Day 4: Tanya was waiting for me with her vampire teeth in a full snarl. I can't help it if I was half an hour late, it took me that long just to tie my shoes. She wanted me to lift dumbbells. Not a chance, Tanya. The word "dumb" is there for a reason. I hid in the men's room until she sent Lars looking for me. As punishment she made me try the rowing machine. It sank.

Day 5: I hate Tanya more than any human being has ever hated any other human being in the history of the world. If there was any part of my body not in extreme pain, I would hit her with it. She thought it would be a good idea to work on my triceps. Well, I have news for you, Tanya, I don't have triceps. And if you don't want dents in the floor, don't hand me any barbells. I refuse to accept responsibility for the damage. You went to sadist school, you are to blame. The treadmill flung me into a science teacher, which hurt. Why couldn't it have been someone softer, like a music teacher?

Day 6: I got Tanya's message on my answering machine, wondering where I am. I lacked the strength to use the TV remote, so I watched eleven straight hours of the weather channel.

Day 7: Thank goodness that's over. Maybe next time my wife will give me something a little more fun, like a gift certificate for a colonoscopy and root canal.

Hockey

Ice hockey fans bring their own pucks to the arena so if necessary, they can throw them at each other – while listening to an organist play songs no one's ever heard before – who come to watch a fight with a chance that a game may break out! In fact, ice hockey is the number one cause of prison riots in North America. Prisoners are locked up in jail watching hockey on TV, and become uncontrollably mad when they see a hockey player get a five-minute penalty for the exact same offense they're doing seventeen years for!

Curling

Apparently two drunk Canadians went into a Yukon bar and decided that if they could combine housework with bowling they could invent a new sport called Curling and make the Olympic team. And the best part about this sport is that they will never be accused of using performance-enhancing drugs!

Bowling

Why is bowling so popular? You put on a polyester shirt with a team name patch on the back like "Morris Meat Company" and a cursive name embroidered on the front. It doesn't even have to be your name, but to be an authentic shirt thought to be coveted by all who dream of putting pink Flamingos in their front yard, it must have a fancy name on the front.

Then you take a big, heavy ball with three holes drilled into it, cram two fingers and a thumb them, take about eight Fred Flintstone twinkle-toe steps, roll the ball, sit down, eat a hot dog, and drink a drink. For this you need special shoes? And when we go to get our shoes, they think we're going to steal them. They make us leave a cash deposit!

Now I don't know about you, but I don't own a green and purple suit that's going to match these goofy shoes, and I definitely don't want to be seen walking around town with an 11 on the back of my foot! And have you heard the television sportscasters cover a bowling match? It's a tough job. "So, Bob, what do you think he should do this time?" "Well, Mary, I think he ought to knock all those pins down and let the air blow on his hand so he can do it again. What do you think?"

Boxing

One year we had an inter-school boxing tournament to raise money for charity. I volunteered to fight a guy, so I needed a trainer/ manager for my corner. I asked a favorite teacher, Coach Ted Weight, to assist me. Round one was brutal as my giant opponent proceeded to rearrange my face. After round one was finally over, I staggered back to my corner all beaten up and dejected. I sat down on the stool, looked up at Coach Weight for some encouragement, and asked, "Did I hit him? Am I doing any damage?" Coach solemnly replied, "No, but keep swinging. Maybe the draft will give him a cold!"

Names

Does it disturb anyone else that "The Los Angeles Angels" baseball team translates directly to "The The Angels Angels"?

Politically Incorrect Team Names?

(This is an email sent to Clarence Page of the Chicago Tribune after an article he published concerning a name change for the Washington Redskins)

Dear Mr. Page: I agree with our Native American population. I am highly insulted by the racially charged name of the Washington Redskins. One might argue that to name a professional football team after Native Americans would exalt them as fine warriors, but nay, nay. We must be careful not to offend, and in the spirit of political correctness and courtesy, we must move forward.

Let's ditch the Kansas City Chiefs, the Atlanta Braves and the Cleveland Indians. If your shorts are in a wad because of the reference the name Redskins makes to skin color, then we need to get rid of the Cleveland Browns. The Carolina Panthers were obviously named to keep the memory of militant Blacks from the 60's alive. Gone. It's offensive to us white folk. The New York Yankees offend the Southern population. Do you see a team named for the Confederacy? No! There is no room for any reference to that tragic war that cost this country so many young men's lives.

I am also offended by the blatant references to the Catholic religion among our sports team names. Totally inappropriate to have the New Orleans Saints, the Los Angeles Angels or the San Diego Padres.

Then there are the team names that glorify criminals who raped and pillaged. We are talking about the Oakland Raiders, the Minnesota Vikings, the Tampa Bay Buccaneers and the Pittsburgh Pirates!

Now, let us address those teams that clearly send the wrong message to our children. The San Diego Chargers promote irresponsible fighting or even spending habits. The wrong message to our children.

The New York Giants and the San Francisco Giants promote obesity, a growing childhood epidemic. The wrong message to our children. The Cincinnati Reds promote downers/barbiturates.

The wrong message to our children. The Milwaukee Brewers. Well, that goes without saying. Another wrong message to our children.

And shouldn't Oregon State also change the name of their women's athletic teams to something other than the "Beavers" - especially when they play Southern California. Do we really want the Trojans sticking it to the Beavers? I'm proud to be a University of Utah 'UTE!'

Rivalry

(No offense intended – insert your own state, cross-town, or school rivalries):

Johnny comes home from his first day of third grade and excitedly reports, "Dad, I was the only guy in the third grade who could count from one to a hundred."

His dad says, "Good job, son. I'm proud. And remember, it's because you're from Arkansas."

Johnny comes home from his second day of school and reports, "Dad, I was the only guy in the third grade who could say his ABCs." His dad says, "Good job, son. It's because you're from Arkansas."

Johnny comes home from school the third day and reports, "Dad, today we had P.E., and the kids wanted to know why I was the only guy in third grade who had hair on my chest, why my feet were so big, and why I was so tall. I proudly told them it was because I was from Arkansas."

His dad said, "No, no, son. It's because you are eighteen!"

Team Support

While I was working security at a football game, a fan spilled beer on a cheerleader's pom-poms. As a favor, I rinsed them off in the men's room. As I shook off the water, someone came out of a stall. Stunned, he announced, "That's the first time anyone's cheered me on while going to the washroom."

A Running Total

An overweight guy is watching TV when a commercial comes on for a guaranteed weight loss of 10 pounds in a week. So, the guy signs up for it. The next morning an incredibly beautiful woman is standing at his door in a bikini, a pair of running shoes and a sign about her neck that reads, "If you can catch me, you can have me."

As soon as he sees her, she takes off running. He tries to catch her but is unable. This continues for a week, at the end of which, the man has lost 10 pounds. So, he signs up for the next weight loss plan - 15 pounds in a week.

The next morning an even more beautiful woman is standing at the door, in similar conditions. The same thing happens for a week, at the end of which he, as suspected, weighs 15 pounds less.

Excited about this success, he decides to do the master program, which requires him to sign a waiver warning about the intensity of this plan. Still he signs up.

The next morning, waiting at the door, is a hulking 300-pound muscular female Russian shot putter wearing a bikini and a pair of running shoes, with a sign around her neck that says,

"If I catch you, you're mine!" The man was supposed to lose 25 pounds in the week, but so far has lost 34 and he's still running!

Speech

A man joins a soccer team, and his new teammates inform him, "At your first team dinner as the new guy, you will have to give us a talk about sex." The evening arrives and he gives a detailed, humorous account of his sex life. When he got home, his wife asked how the evening went and not wanting to lie, but also not wanting to explain exactly what happened, he said, "I had to give a speech about yachting." His wife thought this a little peculiar but said nothing more and went to sleep.

The next day, she bumped into one of his new teammates at the supermarket and asked, "I heard my husband had to give a speech last night. How did it go?"

His mate said, smiling, "It was awesome! Your husband is clearly very experienced!" The wife looked confused and replied, "Strange, he has only done it twice, and the second time he was sick."

Religious Fans

A lot of football fans are the way a lot of people are religious. They didn't read the playbook. They don't know the facts. But they will vehemently defend that their team is the best one, and the other team can burn in hell.

Positive Attitude

I was sitting behind an enthusiastic mom at my son's Little League game. Her boy was pitching for the opposing team and she cheered as he threw wild pitch after wild pitch. The poor kid walked every batter. It was only the first inning, and the score was 14–0. Then one batter finally smacked the ball.

"Oh no," the mom wailed. "There goes his no-hitter."

Lousy Team

Three fans were bemoaning the sorry state of their football team. "I blame the general manager," said the first fan. "If he signed better players, we'd be a great team."

"I blame the players," said the second fan. "If they made more of an effort, we'd score some points."

"I blame my parents," said the third. "If I'd been born in Kansas City, I'd be supporting a decent team."

Bench Warmer

It was the first day of basketball practice at Wingate High School in Brooklyn, N.Y. Coach Johnson handed a ball to each player. "Fellas," he said, "I want you to practice shooting from the spots you might expect to be in during the game."

The No. 12 sub immediately sat down on the bench and began arcing the ball toward the basket.

TV Debate

I was sprawled on the living room couch watching my favorite show on the Food Network when my husband walked in.

"Why do you watch those food shows?" he asked. "You don't even cook."

Glaring back at him, I asked, "Then why do you watch football?"

Female Perspective

Anyone who thinks women talk too much has never sat through a six-hour Super Bowl pregame show! The reason women don't play football is that 11 of them would never wear the same outfit in public. But women prefer the tight yoga pants football players wear over the frumpy businesswoman slacks baseball players wear!

Female Fan

A first-grade teacher can't believe her female student isn't fired up about the Stanley Cup. "It's a huge event. Why aren't you excited?"

"Because I'm not a hockey fan. My parents love basketball, so I do too," says the student.

"Well, that's a lousy reason," says the teacher. "What if your parents were morons? What would you be then?"

"The young girl blurted, "Then I'd be a hockey fan."

Little League Umpire

One summer, I worked as a Little League umpire. During one game, a nine-year-old rookie came up to bat against an all-star pitcher who was twelve. The pitcher took a mighty wind-up, reared back, and threw a fastball.

"Strike," I called.

The young batter whined, "C'mon, ump, that wasn't a strike." I said, "Why? Did you see it?"

He replied, "No, but it sounded high."

Extra Credit

Two college basketball players were flunking a class and needed some extra credit points to be eligible for that night's game. The professor explained, "If you can answer one question, you will pass and play tonight. The question is: 'Old McDonald had a ___.' I'll be back in a minute for your written responses."

The professor left, and after ten minutes of tense silence, one player grabbed his head and said to the other, "What is the answer?"

"Are you serious?" the other replied. It's easy. Old McDonald had a farm."

"Oh yeah, I remember!" He went to write it down but paused. "How do you spell farm?"

The other player couldn't believe it. "You idiot. It's easy: E-I-E-I-O!"

Unconscious

Standing on the sidelines, during a game being played by my school's football team, I saw one of the players take a hard hit. He tumbled to the ground and didn't move.

We grabbed our first-aid gear and rushed out onto the field. The coach picked up the young man's hand and urged, "Son, can you hear me? Squeeze once for yes and twice for no."

End Zone

Anyone who's just driven 90 yards against huge men trying to kill them has earned the right to do a dance anywhere he chooses without being penalized!

Bear

Two men were hiking when they came face to face with a bear. The bear was startled, the men were startled, the bear got mad, and the men turned and began running down the mountain trail. Suddenly, one man stopped, which caused the other man to stop.

"Why are you stopping?" asked one man. "To put on my running shoes," the other replied. "Why? You can't outrun the bear," he countered. "I know. All I have to do is outrun you!"

GOLF

Books

Have you ever known someone who plays so much golf that he actually gathers his friends together to show them slides of work? Because I love golf I decided to write two new books about my personal experiences:

"How To Line Up Your Fifth Putt"

"Awesome Second Shots Off The Ladies Tee"

Caddy Comebacks

Golfer: Think I'll drown myself in the lake.
Caddy: Don't think you can keep your head down that long!

Golfer: Do you think I can get there with a 5 iron?
Caddy: Eventually!

Golfer: Stop checking your watch. It's distracting.
Caddy: It's not a watch, sir, it's a compass!

Golfer: How do you like my game?
Caddy: Good sir, but I prefer golf!

Golfer: That can't be my ball. It's too old.
Caddy: It's been a long time since we teed off sir!

Celebrity Golf

I'm not a great golfer. Last year I had my ball-retriever re-gripped! The first time I played in a celebrity golf tournament it took so long that my clothes had gone out of style by the time we finished eighteen holes.

I should have known it was going to be a long day when I lost my first ball in the ball washer! It was finally my turn to hit, and when I reared back and took my mighty swing, I whiffed and completely missed the ball. Embarrassed I took a second swing and whiffed again. Frustrated, I took a third mighty swing and missed, but this time my club blew the ball off the tee! As I bent over to place my ball back onto the tee, the starter made me relax and everybody else laugh when he commented, "Tough course, isn't it?"

I was playing so poorly that day that I had to wait until I hit it before I knew which course I was playing. When I finally did get a hold of one, I hit a man right in the back who was so mad that he pulled off the highway and came and found me!

As we walked along the eighteenth hole, I apologized to my caddy, acknowledging that I knew he was exhausted." Quietly he replied, "Actually we've been out here so long I'm homesick!"

As I laughed, I commented to the course marshal who had been following us, "Boy oh boy, this is a tough course."

The marshal winced, "Actually, sir, you haven't been on it for over an hour!"

Outdoorsy Man

During his physical, the doctor asked the patient about his daily activity level. He described a typical day this way: "Well, yesterday afternoon, I waded along the edge of a lake, drank eight beers, escaped from wild dogs in the heavy brush, jumped away from an aggressive rattlesnake, marched up and down several rocky hills, stood in a patch of poison ivy, crawled out of quicksand and took four leaks behind big trees."

Inspired by the story, the doctor said, "You must be one heck of an outdoorsman!" "Nah," he replied, "I'm just a lousy golfer!"

Tee Box

It was a sunny Sunday morning, and Murray was beginning his pre-shot routine, visualizing his upcoming shot, when a voice came over the clubhouse loudspeaker. "Would the gentleman on the ladies' tee please back up to the men's tee."

Murray remained in his routine, seemingly unfazed by the interruption. A little louder: "Would the man on the women's tee kindly back up to the men's tee?"

Murray raised up out of his stance, lowered his driver, and shouted, "Would the announcer in the clubhouse kindly shut up and let me hit my second shot?"

Finding Balls

One golfer from the foursome arrived at the 19th Hole thirty minutes after his buddies. When they asked him why, he showed them a huge bruise on his neck and answered in an unrecognizable, raspy voice while he gasped for air: "When I hit my tee shot into the woods and told you guys to go ahead and keeping playing, I immediately started searching for my Nike. Before long, I heard a moaning cow, and noticed it had something shiny and reflecting from her backside. Carefully I lifted up her tail and sure enough she had a golf ball stuck in her butt. Sadly, it was not my Nike.

Just then a golf cart pulled up with two women in it. One asked me if I had seen her Pink Callaway. Without thinking I turned to the cow, lifted up the tail, and pointing to the butt asked, "Does this look anything like yours?" And she hit me across my neck with her five iron!"

Loft

Three guys are golfing with the club pro. First guy tees off and hits a dribbler about sixty yards. He turns to the pro and says, "What did I do wrong?"

The pro says, "LOFT."

The next guy tees off and hits a duck hook into the woods. He asks the pro, "What did I do wrong?"

The pro says, "LOFT."

The third guy tees off and hits a slice into a pond. He asks the pro, "What did I do wrong?"

The pro says, "LOFT."

As they are walking to their balls, the first guy finally speaks up. He says to the pro, "The three of us hit completely different tee shots, and when we asked you what we did wrong, you gave each of us the same exact answer each time. What is a loft?"
The pro says, "Lack Of Flippin' Talent."

Unmarried

Three unmarried men were waiting to tee off when the

starter walked up to them and said, "You see that beautiful blonde practicing her putting?"

"Her? Wow, she is beautiful," they all said.

"She is a good golfer," he continued," and would like to hook up with a group. None of the other groups will play with a woman. Can she play with you? She won't hold you up, I promise." They looked at each other and said, "Sure! She can join us." Just as the starter said, the woman played well and kept up. Plus, they kept noticing how attractive she was.

When they reached the 18th hole, she said that if she sank her 18-foot putt, she would break 80 for the first time. And because she was single and wanted to marry a man who loves golf as much as she did, whichever one of them helped her read the putt correctly, which helped her make it, she would marry him!"

All three jumped at the chance. The first one looked over the putt and said, "I see it breaking 10 inches left to right." The second looked it over from all sides and said, "No, I see it breaking eight inches right to left."

The third man looked at the woman, looked at the ball, and said, "Pick it up. It's good!"

Abraham And Moses

Abraham and Moses were playing golf. They came to a

par-three hole. Moses stepped up to hit the ball and his caddy said, "Use a six iron."

Moses asked, "What would Arnold Palmer use?" The caddy answered, "A nine iron."

Moses pulled out his nine iron and hit the ball right into the water. The gallery of backed-up, delayed golfers moaned as they watched him lay down his club, walk out and part the water, pick up his ball, walk back, and tee it up again. His caddy again handed him a six iron, but Moses said, "No, hand me my nine."

Again, he hit it into the water. He threw down his club, walked again down to the pond, and parted the water to retrieve his ball. While he was gone, a disgruntled golfer in the foursome behind them yelled, "Hey, who does this guy think he is, God?"

The caddy turned and answered, "No, sir. He thinks he's Arnold Palmer!"

Truth Be Told

John, who lived in the north of England, decided to go golfing in Scotland with his buddy, Shawn. So, they loaded up John's minivan and headed north. After driving for a few hours, they got caught in a terrible blizzard. I realized it's terrible weather out there and I have this huge house all to myself, but I'm recently widowed, she explained, and I'm afraid the neighbors will talk if I let you stay in my house.

"Don't worry," John said. "We will be happy to sleep in the barn. And if the weather breaks, we will be gone at first light."

The lady agreed, and the two men found their way to the barn and settled in for the night.

Come morning, the weather had cleared, and they got on their way. They enjoyed a great weekend of golf.

But about nine months later, John got an unexpected letter from an attorney. It took him a few minutes to figure it out, but he finally determined that it was from the attorney of that attractive widow he had met on the golf weekend.

He dropped in on his friend Shawn and asked, "Shawn, do you remember that good-looking widow from the farm we stayed at on our golf holiday in Scotland about 9 months ago?"

"Yes, I do," said Shawn.

"Did you happen to get up in the middle of the night, go up to the house, and pay her a visit?"

"Well, um, yes!" Shawn said, a little embarrassed about being found out, "I have to admit that I did."

"And did you happen to give her my name instead of telling her your name?"

Shawn's face turned beet red and he said, "Yeah, look, I'm sorry, buddy. I'm afraid I did. Why do you ask?"

"She just died and left me everything!"

Best Golf Signs

"It takes a lot of balls to golf like I do."

"Years ago, when men cursed and beat the ground with sticks it was called 'witchcraft.' Today it's known as golf."

"You are 100 yards from the center of the green. You are 175 yards from a $200 plate glass window. Choose your club carefully."

"Please don't lick your balls. The fairways have been sprayed with insecticides."

"Golfers Parking Only - violators will be clubbed."

"Wanted Good Woman! Must be able to clean, cook, sew, caddy, and find lost balls. Must have golf cart and trailer. Please send picture of golf cart and trailer."

"No Trespassing - Don't even think about coming onto this field unless you can run a 4.6 forty-yard dash. My mean and crazy bull can do it in 4.1."

Confession

A man goes into the confessional. "Forgive me, Father, for I have sinned."

"What is your sin, my child?" the priest replies.

"I used some horrible language this week, and I feel absolutely terrible."

"When did you use this awful language?" asks the priest.

"I was golfing and hit a drive that looked like it was going to go over 250 yards, but it struck a phone line and fell straight down to the ground."

"Is that when you swore?"

"No, Father," says the man. "An eagle came down out of the sky, grabbed the ball in its talons, and began to fly away!"

"Is that when you swore?" asked the amazed priest.

"No, not yet," the man replies. "As the eagle flew toward the green, the ball fell, struck a tree, bounced through some bushes, careened off a big rock, and rolled through a sand trap onto the green and stopped within six inches of the hole."

The priest sighs. "Now I see. You missed the damn putt, didn't you?"

Harry

Noting that her husband looked more haggard and disgruntled than usual after his weekly golf game, his wife asked what was wrong.

He answered, "Well, on the fourth hole, my friend Harry had a heart attack and died. It was terrible! The entire rest of the day, it was hit the ball, drag Harry, hit the ball, drag Harry!"

The Barn

A man and his wife are playing the fifth hole at their club when he slices his drive so far to the right it rolls into an equipment barn. He finds the ball and plans to take a drop when she says, "Let me go down to the other end of the barn and hold the door open. Then you can hit your ball through the door and back to the fairway."

He thinks this is a good idea, so she holds the door. He takes a big swing, but rather than flying through the door, the ball hits her in the head and kills her.

A year later, the same man and his new bride are playing the same hole when he again slices the ball into the shed. He finds it and plans to take an unplayable lie when she says, "Let me go down to the other end of the barn and hold the door open. Then you can hit your ball through the door and back to the fairway."

He looks at her, shakes his head, and explains, "No way. The last time I tried that, I took a triple bogey on this hole!"

African Course

An avid golfer was in Africa where he was driven deep into the jungle to the course. His caddie was waiting on the first tee with a bagful of clubs under one arm and a rifle under the other.

The golfer hit a good drive down the fairway of the opening hole, a tough par four. As they were walking to his ball, a tiger sprang out of the rough and charged the golfer. Without missing a beat, the caddie dropped the bag, aimed his rifle, and shot the animal dead.

Startled, the golfer had to compose himself, but quickly recovered, hit a good approach, and parred the hole.

The same thing happened on the second hole. But this time a lion bolted out of the jungle, charged the golfer, and was dropped by a single shot from the caddie's rifle.

By now, the golfer was visibly shaken, but continued to play the third hole, a par three surrounded by water. The golfer hit it three feet from the cup. As he was walking onto the green, a crocodile slid out of the water and began moving toward him.

Unfazed, the golfer looked to his caddie for help. But the caddie stood motionless. The crocodile moved closer, and the golfer again glanced at the caddie, who didn't move. Finally, with the crocodile just inches away, the golfer screamed, "Aren't you going to do something?"

The caddie looked at the scorecard and said, "I'm sorry, sir, but you don't get a shot on this hole." Ha!

Dilemma

You are playing for the Club Championship. Your opponent is the cockiest, most arrogant member whom everyone despises. Going into the seventeenth hole, you are tied, and you have 'Honors.' You tee off and hit it 300 yards down the middle of the fairway. He tees off and hits it into the trees. You both spend ten minutes looking for his ball, when he tells you to go hit your second shot, and he will meet you on the green. After you hit your ball eight feet from the hole, you hear, "Found it!" Suddenly, a ball comes sailing out of the trees and lands on the green one foot from the hole for a 'gimme.' Here is the dilemma: Do you take the lying, cheating bum's ball out of your pocket and confront him with it? Or do you just keep your mouth shut?

Altar

As a couple approaches the altar, the groom tells his wife-to-be, "Honey, I've got something to confess: I'm a golf nut, and every chance I get, I'll be playing golf!"

"Since we're being honest," replies the bride, "I have to tell you that I'm a hooker."

The groom replies, "That's okay, honey. You just need to learn to keep your head down and your left arm straight!"

Worst

A pathetic golfer was getting frustrated with his lousy game and began blaming his mistakes on his caddie.

As the round came to an end, the golfer said, "You have to be the worst caddie in the whole wide world."

To which the caddie replied, "I don't think so, sir. That would be too much of a coincidence."

Hospital

There is a golf course where the parking lot is just to the right of the first fairway. Separating the fairway and lot is the access road to the pro shop.

One day, a ball comes flying off the first tee, hits the rear window of one car and shatters it, ricochets into the windshield of another car and cracks that, then bounces and hits a golfer in the head as he is unloading his clubs. He has to be taken to the hospital.

After surveying the damage, the golf pro asks each golfer as he walks off the ninth green if anyone hit a slice of the first tee. After numerous negative replies, the pro finally finds his culprit. The golfer admits that, yes, indeed, he hit his first tee shot to the right, but it went out-of-bounds, he and the rest of his group didn't bother looking for it.

The pro explains about the two car windows and the golfer in the hospital. By the time he finishes re-creating the scene, the entire foursome is visibly upset, and the golfer who hit the errant shot moans, "Oh, that's terrible. What can I do?"

The pro says, "You should probably try rolling your hands a little to the right to strengthen your grip."

A Religious Advantage

Jesus, Moses, and an elderly gentleman are playing golf. Moses hits his drive into the pond, and his ball sinks to the bottom. Moses heads for the pond, parts the water, hits his ball onto the green. Jesus says, "Nice shot Moses." Jesus then hits his drive into the same pond. The ball is sitting on the water. Jesus walks on the water and hits his ball onto the green. Moses says, "You too, Jesus. Fine shot." The elderly gentleman steps up and hits his drive 40 yards for the worst shot of the day. A huge wind gust pushes the ball into the pond. A large carp leaps out of the water with the ball in its mouth. A hawk swoops down out of the sky to grab the fish, flies 350 yards down the fairway, and drops the ball onto the green. A squirrel runs out of the woods and nudges the ball into the cup for a hole-in-one. Jesus says, "Nice shot Dad!"

Interesting...

Golf balls are like eggs. They're white, sold by the dozen, and a week later you have to buy some more.

After a poor round, a golfer despondently walked up the 18th and said, "I've played so badly all day, I think I'm going to drown myself in that lake." The caddie, quick as a flash, replied, "I'm not sure you could keep your head down that long."

I thought I knew all the terminology of golf. But when I overheard some old guys talking about their game, I had to ask the pro what a 'rider' was. The pro said, "A rider is when you hit the ball far enough to actually get in the golf cart and ride to it."

When your round of golf is interrupted by a lightning

storm just hold your 1-iron above your head, because even God can't hit a 1-iron.

Do you know why there are 18 holes on a golf course? Because that's how long it took the Scotts who invented the game to finish their bottle of whiskey!

A guy in our foursome today crushed his tee shot and my caddie blurted, "Whoa bro. I don't even drive that far on vacation!"

I hit my ball on the green and was putting a four-footer for birdie. When I left it a foot short, my playing partner said, "Good lag, and you definitely had the right club!"

TRAVEL COMEDY

Airport

If you can't afford a doctor, go to an airport - you'll get a free X-ray and a body massage, and if you mention Al Qaeda, you'll get a free colonoscopy!

If flying is so safe, why is the airport called a 'terminal'?

Confusing Traffic Signs

A police officer pulls over a carload of nuns and says, "Sister, this is a 65 MPH highway — why are you going so slow?"

Sister: "Sir, I saw a lot of signs that said 22, not 65."

Officer: "Oh sister, that's not the speed limit, that's the name of the highway you're on!"

Sister: "Oh, Silly me! Thanks for letting me know. I'll be more careful."

At this point the officer looks in the backseat and sees that the other nuns are shaking and trembling. "Excuse me, Sister, what's wrong with your friends back there?"

Sister: "Oh, we just got off of highway 119!"

Airport Shuttle

The shuttle is the worst $20 you'll ever save. It adds 90 minutes to whatever a Town Car or cab would have been. You have the unenviable choice between being dropped off last or being dropped off first and having a bunch of losers who can't afford cab fare and have no friends or loved ones with cars knowing exactly where you live.

Fear

My fear of flying starts as soon as I buckle myself in and then the guy up front mumbles a few unintelligible words then before I know it I'm thrust into the back of my seat by the acceleration that seems way too fast and the rest of the trip is an endless nightmare of turbulence, of near misses.... and then the taxi driver drops me off at the airport.

Flight Delays

People say there are delays on flights. Delays, really?

New York to California in five hours, that used to take 30 years, a bunch of people used to die on the way there, have a baby, and you would end up with a whole different group of people by the time you got there. Now you watch a movie and go to the toilet and you are home. STOP complaining!

Taxi Driver

A woman and her 12-year-old son were riding in a taxi in Detroit. It was raining and all the prostitutes were standing under awnings. "Mom," said the boy, "What are all those women doing?"

"They're waiting for their husbands to get off work," she replied.

The taxi driver turns around and says, "Geez lady, why don't you tell him the truth? They're hookers, boy! They have sex with men for money."

The little boy's eyes get wide and he says, "Is that true Mom?" His mother, glaring hard at the driver, answers "yes."

After a few minutes the kid asks, "Mom, if those women have babies, what happens to them?"

She said, "Most of them become taxi drivers!"

Hotels

Have you ever stayed at one of those low-budget, no-tell motels trying to save money? They want us to feel at home and welcome, and we do, until we get into our room. Suddenly, we feel violated. Everything is screwed down! You can't even pick up the remote control. You have to aim it and shoot. Even the pictures are screwed to the wall. This intrigues me. Why do they think we want to steal pictures of wheat? I prefer the hotels where the towels in your room are so fluffy you have a hard time getting your suitcase closed.

Flight Attendant

Because I have flown over six million miles just on Delta Airlines, and have survived a plane crash, just once I wish the flight attendants would give me the microphone to give my version of the pre-flight safety demonstration: 'In the event of an emergency a little gold cup is going to conk you on the head. When you stop screaming brace yourself for a 200 feet-per-second vertical dive. And if you are traveling with more than one child, pick your favorite! And no, you don't have to bring your seats up to the most upright and uncomfortable position, because if we crash, an inch and a half is not going to make a difference!"

Yes, we could crash, but it beats driving – and yes flying is fun. On one Delta flight we were coming in for a landing at the Dallas/Fort Worth airport, when our jet hit heavy turbulence and bounced all over the sky. When we finally touched down, we hit loud and hard, bounced, hit again, bounced, and hit a third time, this time staying on the ground.

As we taxied to the gate, the flight attendant spoke over the public address system, "Welcome to Dallas, Texas. If you enjoyed your flight, tell your friends you flew Delta. If you did not enjoy your flight, tell your friends you flew Southwest.

And please remain seated with your seat belt fastened tightly while Captain Kangaroo bounces our plane to the terminal."

As we got off the plane, the elderly woman walking in front of me stopped the pilot and asked, "Did we really land, or did we get shot down?"

The Polite Pilot

I was flying from San Francisco to Los Angeles. By the time we took off, there had been a forty-five-minute delay and everybody on board was angry. Unexpectedly, we stopped in Sacramento on the way. The flight attendant explained that there would be another forty-five-minute delay, and if we wanted to get off the aircraft, we would re-board in thirty minutes.

Everybody got off the plane except one gentleman who was blind. I had noticed him as I walked by and could tell he had flown before because his seeing-eye dog lay quietly underneath the seats in front of him throughout the entire flight. I could also tell he had flown this very flight before because the pilot approached him and calling him by name, said, "Keith, we're here in Sacramento for almost an hour. Would you like to get off and stretch your legs?"

Keith replied, "No thanks, but maybe my dog would like to stretch his legs."

Picture this: All the people in the gate area came to a complete standstill when they looked up and saw the pilot walk off the plane with a seeing-eye dog. The pilot was even wearing sunglasses! People scattered. They not only tried to change planes, but they were also trying to change airlines!

The Ultimate Airline Saga

I was flying from Chicago to Springfield, Illinois, on a commuter airline. It was on one of those forty-passenger prop jobs where you buy your ticket from the commuter counter, leave from a United Airlines gate, and pass by the pilot who is wearing an American Airlines hat.

While waiting in line at the ticket counter, the man in front of me cracked me up when he said, "I want my luggage to go to Jamaica and I want to go to Albuquerque." The ticket lady said, "I'm sorry, but we can't do that."

The man replied, "Why? You did it last time!"

We took off, and the flight attendant served the usual little toy meals with plugged toy salt and pepper shakers and toy utensils. The food was an upgrade from the usual rubber chicken surprise, but I didn't eat it because the chunk of beef was so red and rare that a good veterinarian could have probably brought it back to life.

The longer we flew, the more I realized they shouldn't just have no smoking sections on airplanes, they should have no talking sections. For some reason, when certain people get their bodies into any kind of reclining position, they think it is automatic therapy and want to tell you their entire life story, beginning with DNA.

The guy next to me was hairy—I mean he had hair where most monkeys don't. And of course, he was wearing a stinky tank top (for some reason hairy guys always want to show us their hair) with a vulgar slogan printed on the front of his shirt. This kills me. If I don't want to hear from this guy's mouth, why should I want to hear from his clothing?

I got off the plane and went into the terminal to retrieve my bags. Wouldn't you know it—they lost my luggage.

As I filled out the paperwork, I overheard an elderly southern lady tearing into the man across the counter. "Don't you lie to me, don't you dare lie to me! I know that if the pilot of this plane can fly in the dark and can find Springfield Illinois in a snowstorm, then you can find my bag!"

Another man was standing on the other side of me with his suitcase beside him on the floor. It was plastered with stickers, which read Hawaii, Toronto, Oklahoma, Utah and Florida. Seeing the suitcase, the elderly woman blurted out, "My, oh my, have you been to all those places?"

The man replied, "No, but my luggage has!"

Plane Time

The first time I flew from Atlanta, Georgia to Montgomery, Alabama I had no idea about this specific time zone change. The clerk at the counter said, "The plane leaves at 12 noon, and you arrive one minute earlier in Montgomery at 11:59 am. Would you like to buy a ticket?" Bewildered I replied, "Heck no, I don't want a ticket. But I sure want to see the plane take off!"

Help Desk

A woman called our airline customer-service desk asking if she could take her dog on board.

"Sure," I said, "as long as you provide your own kennel." I further explained that the kennel needed to be large enough for the dog to stand up, sit down, turn around, and rollover.

The customer was flummoxed: "I'll never be able to teach him all of that by tomorrow!"

Seat Humor

Have you seen the safety instruction card on most airlines? In the emergency exit row the card says, "If you cannot read this, please notify the flight attendant and she will change your seat assignment. And what about the Delta Airlines sickness bag? To save money, they have combined two signs. On one side of the bag, it says: For Motion Discomfort. On the other side it says: Occupied. Apparently, you can throw up in the bag and then leave it on your seat so no one sits there while you're gone!

Engine Trouble

One day, I was on an airplane, a three-engine 727 jet. I never get nervous until I start thinking about how the plane has over thirty thousand moving parts put together by the lowest bidder. We were circling the Denver airport when the plane suddenly dipped and jolted to the left. The pilot came on the public address system, "I'm sorry, we have lost the left engine and will have to climb to gain some altitude. There will be a ten-minute delay."

About nine minutes went by, and suddenly the plane jolted to the right. The pilot came back on the speaker. "We just lost the right engine and have to climb to gain some additional altitude. There will be another fifteen-minute delay."

Hearing this, the man sitting next to me leaned over and very solemnly said, "I sure hope we don't lose that last engine, or we could be up here all day!"

When we finally landed, we screeched to an abrupt halt. Since I was on the front row, I overheard the conversation between the pilot and the copilot. The pilot said, "Man, this runway is short!"

The copilot replied, "Yeah, but it's about two miles wide!" (Gotcha!)

Flight Lead

My flight was being served by a flight attendant, who was obviously gay, and who put everyone in a good mood as he served us food and drinks.

As the plane prepared to descend, he came swishing down the aisle and explained, "Captain Marvey has asked me to announce that he'll be landing the big scary plane shortly, so lovely people, if you could just put your trays up, that would be super."

On his way back up the aisle, he noticed this well-dressed man hadn't moved a muscle. "Perhaps you didn't hear me over those big brute engines, but I asked you to raise your trazy-poo, so the main man can pitty-pat us on the ground."

He calmly turned his head and said with an accent, "In my country, I am called a Prince - Prince Richard, and I take orders from no one."

To which the flight attendant replied, without missing a beat, "Well, sweet-pecks, in my country I'm called a Queen, so I outrank you. Tray-up, Royal Jerk!"

Cultural Fun

I checked into a hotel in San Jose, California. The gentleman working at the front desk had on a nametag that read J-O-S-E. I said, "Nice to meet you Geosee."

He smiled and said, "No sir, it's Hozay - like "Hozay Can You See."

I said, "That's funny. This is a beautiful city, San Geosee."

He laughed and again corrected me, "No, no, it's San

Hozay. When you come and visit us again?"

With tongue in cheek I answered, "Oh, sometime between Hune and Huly!"

Chinese English

A Chinese airliner tragically crashed into a mountain. The pilot's name: "We Too Low." Co-pilot's name: "Some Ting Wong." Flight engineer's name: "What Went Wong." Flight attendant's name: "Pull up Now." Investigator's report: "Two wongs don't make a wight!"

Twisted Drivers

When all the freeway shootings were taking place in California, I saw a bumper sticker, "Honk if you're reloading." Everyone was suddenly gracious and polite. "No, please, you go first. No. I can't. You go in front of me. Please. No. You pull in." The person you let in flipped you the peace sign and the person you made wait behind you flipped you a half a peace sign!

Pronunciation

Two men were driving through Louisiana. As they were

approaching Natchidoches, they started arguing about the pronunciation of the town. They argued back and forth until they stopped for lunch.

As they stood at the counter, one asked the female employee, "Before we order, could you settle a twenty-dollar bet for us? Would you please pronounce where we are... very slowly?"

The lady leaned over the counter and said, "Burrr Gerrr Kiiiing."

Cow

After crawling along at a pitifully slow pace for miles, a passenger train finally stopped. Seeing the guard walking along the track, a passenger leaned out the window and asked: "What's going on?"

"There's a cow on the track," replied the guard. Ten minutes later, the train moved off and resumed its slow pace, but within five minutes it had stopped again. The passenger saw the same guard walking past outside once more and asked him: "What happened? Did we catch up with the cow again?"

Fast Biking

A man decided that he was going to ride a 10-speed

bike from Phoenix to Flagstaff. He got as far as Black Canyon City before the mountains just became too much and he could go no farther.

He stuck his thumb out, but after 3 hours hadn't gotten a single person to stop. Finally, a guy in a Corvette pulled over and offered him a ride. Of course, the bike wouldn't fit in the car. The owner of the Corvette found a piece of rope lying by the highway and tied it to his bumper. He tied the other end to the bike and told the man that if he was going too fast, to honk the horn on his bike and that he would slow down.

Everything went fine for the first 30 miles. Suddenly, another Corvette blew past them. Not to be outdone, the Corvette pulling the bike took off after the other. A short distance down the road the Corvettes, both going well over 120 mph, blew through a speed trap.

The police officer noted the speeds from his radar gun and radioed to the other officer that he had two Corvettes headed his way at over 120 mph. He then relayed, "and there's a guy on a 10-speed bike honking to pass.

He's teaching her arithmetic
He said it was his mission,
He kissed her once, he kissed her twice
And said, "Now that's addition."

And as he added smack by smack
In silent satisfaction,
She sweetly gave the kisses back
And said, "Now that's subtraction."

Then he kissed her, she kissed him
Without an explanation,
Then both together smiled and said,
"That's multiplication."

Then Dad appeared upon the scene
And made a quick decision,
He kicked that kid three blocks away
And said, "That's long–division!"

OUTRAGEOUS LETTERS

The Water Closet

An English lady was looking to rent a room in Switzerland and asked the local village schoolmaster to help her. A place that suited her was finally found, and the lady returned to London for her belongings. She remembered that she had not noticed a toilet/washroom, or as she called it, a 'Water Closet,' so she wrote to the schoolmaster. He was puzzled by the initials W.C., never dreaming, of course, that she was asking about a toilet/ washroom. He finally asked the parish priest who decided that W.C. stood for Westbrook Church. This was his reply:

Dear Madam,

The W.C. is situated nine miles from the house in the center of a beautiful grove of trees. It is capable of holding 350 people at a time and is open on Tuesday, Thursday, and Sunday each week. A large number of folks attend during the summer months, so it is suggested you go early, although there is plenty of standing room. Some folks like to take their lunch and make a day of it, especially on Thursday when there is organ accompaniment.

It may be of interest to you to know that my daughter met her husband in the W.C. and was also married there. We hope you will be there in time for our bazaar to be held very soon. The proceeds will go toward the purchase of plush seats, which the folks agree are a long-felt need, as the present seats all have holes in them.

I close now with the desire to accommodate you in every way possible, and I will be happy to save you a seat down front or near the door, whichever you prefer. Sincerely, Schoolmaster

Letter From Camp

Dear Mom,

Our scoutmaster told us all to write to our parents in case you saw the flood on TV and worried. We are OK. Only one of our tents and two sleeping bags got washed away. Luckily, none of us got drowned because we were all up on the mountain looking for Chad when it happened.

Oh yes, please call Chad's mother and tell her he is OK. He can't write because of the cast. I got to ride in one of the search and rescue Jeeps. It was neat. We never would have found him in the dark if hadn't been for the lightning. Scoutmaster Webb got mad at Chad for going on a hike alone without telling anyone. Chad said he did tell him, but it was during the fire so he probably didn't hear him.

Did you know that if you put a gas can on a fire, it will blow up? The wet wood still didn't burn, but one of our tents did, also some of our clothes. John is going to look weird until his hair grows back. We will be home on Saturday if Scoutmaster Webb gets the car fixed.

It wasn't his fault about the wreck. The brakes worked OK when we left. Scoutmaster Webb said that with a car that old you have to expect something to break down; that's probably why he can't get insurance on it. We think it's a neat car. He doesn't care if we get it dirty, and if it's hot, sometimes he lets us ride on the tailgate, and it gets pretty hot with ten people in a car. He let us take turns riding in the trailer until the highway patrolman stopped and talked to us.

Scoutmaster Webb is a neat guy. Don't worry, he is a good driver. In fact, he is teaching Terry how to drive. But he only lets him drive on the mountain roads where there isn't any traffic.

All we ever see up there are logging trucks. This morning all of the guys were diving off the rocks and swimming out in the lake. Scoutmaster Webb wouldn't let me because I can't swim and Chad was afraid he would sink because of his cast, so he let us take the canoe across the lake. It was great. You can still see some of the trees under the water from the flood.

Scoutmaster Webb isn't crabby like some scoutmasters.

He didn't even get mad about the life jackets. He has to spend a lot of time working on the car so we are trying not to cause him any trouble.

Guess what? We have all passed our first-aid merit badges. When Dave dove in the lake and cut his arm, we got to see how a tourniquet works. Also Wade and I threw up. Scoutmaster Webb said it probably was just food poisoning from the leftover chicken. He said they got sick that way with the food they ate in prison. I'm so glad he got out and became our scoutmaster. He said he sure figured out how to get things done better while he was doing his time. I have to go now. We are going into town to mail our letters and buy bullets. Don't worry about anything. We are fine. Love, Cole

Freshman's First Letter Home

Dear Mom,

I'm sorry it's taken me so long to write. I've never been to the city before. It's my first time away from you, and I'm trying to figure everything out. I don't live where I did when you dropped me off. I read in the paper where most accidents happen within twenty miles of where you live, so I moved.

This place has what I thought was a washing machine. The first day I put four shirts in it, I pulled the chain and haven't seen them since. I finally found the real machine and bought laundry detergent. It said "ALL," so I dumped the whole box in. I now owe three thousand dollars for flood damage, but they deducted three hundred dollars because the carpets on all three floors of the dorms are clean!

It only rained twice this week—three days the first time and four days the second time. The president of my fraternity fell in a whiskey vat at our last party. Some students tried to pull him out, but he fought them off gallantly and drowned. We cremated him, but couldn't get the flame to go out. He burned for five days.

Three of my other friends went off a bridge in a pick-up. One was driving. The other two were in the back. The driver got out. He rolled down the window and swam to safety. The other two drowned because they couldn't get the tailgate down. Sincerely, Your Loving Son

Family Ties

Dear Abby,

I have two brothers. One is a motivational speaker, and the other one was sent to the electric chair. I have two sisters. One is a well-known prostitute and the other is a Communist working to overthrow the government. My mom is in an insane asylum, and the five men claiming to be my father are all drug dealers. I just met a wonderful man who will soon be released from prison for the double ax murders of his parents. We are very much in love and plan to marry. My problem—do you think he will still marry me if I tell him about my brother who is a motivational speaker?

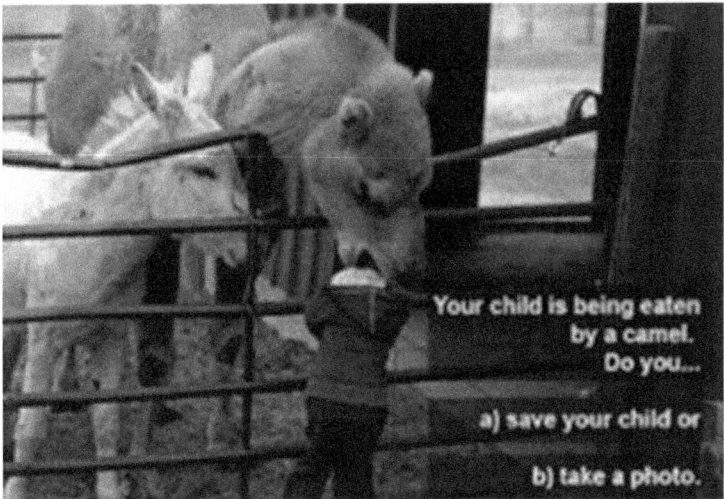

Your child is being eaten by a camel. Do you...

a) save your child or

b) take a photo.

FAMILY FUNNIES

Truth

If you love something, set it free. If it comes back, it was and always will be yours. If it never returns, it was never yours to begin with. If it just sits in your living room, messes up your stuff, eats your food, uses your telephone, takes your money, and never behaves as if you actually set it free in the first place... you most likely gave birth to it.

Genealogy

A child asked his father, "How were people born?" So, his father said, "Adam and Eve made babies, then their babies became adults and made babies, and so on." The child then went to his mother, asked her the same question and she told him, "We were monkeys then we evolved to become like we are now." The child ran back to his father and said, "You lied to me!" His father replied, "No, your mom was talking about her side of the family."

Parents Boredom

What did our parents do to kill boredom before the internet? I asked my 26 brothers and sisters and they didn't know either!

Honest Confusion

A preacher was presenting a children's Easter sermon and knew that asking questions was both crucial and dangerous. When he asked if they knew the meaning of the resurrection, a little boy raised his hand and blurted, "I know that if you have a resurrection that lasts more than four hours you are supposed to call the doctor." It took over ten minutes for the congregation to settle down enough for the service to continue.

More Confusion

At a church testimony meeting where members can stand at the pulpit and share their gratitude and conviction, an elderly woman stepped to the microphone and said, "I want to thank all of you for your faith and prayers during this difficult time. My husband has been bed-ridden for weeks, but I was able to provide comfort by gently rubbing his scrotum."

The congregation gasped and laughed. As she left the pulpit to take her seat, her husband passed her in a sprint to the microphone. He said, "Brothers and sisters, that is sternum. She rubbed my sternum to give me relief!"

When he sat back down his wife loudly blurted, "Scrotum? I said scrotum?" And ran red-faced out of the chapel to drive straight home!

High Birth Rate

A little rural town had one of the highest birth rates in the country. This phenomenon attracted the attention of the sociologists at the state university. They wrote a grant proposal, got a huge chunk of money, moved to town, set up their computers, and began designing their questionnaires.

While the staff was busy getting ready for their big research effort, the project director went to the local drugstore for a cup of coffee. He sat down at the counter, ordered his coffee, and while he was drinking it, he told the druggist what his purpose was in town. He then asked him if he had any idea why the birth rate was so high.

"Sure," said the druggist. "Every morning the six o'clock train comes through town and blows its horn for the crossing. It wakes everybody up, and, well, it's too late to go back to sleep and it's too early to get up!"

Insecurity

The other day someone came up to me after my speech and asked, "Why do you need all this attention? Are you insecure?" Then I started thinking, I guess I am insecure; my whole life I've wondered whethers I was adopted. Now, obviously, there's nothing wrong with being adopted. I just think your parents should tell you when the time is right. So, after all these years of insecurity and wonder, I finally got up enough courage to ask my father if I was adopted. I walked into his room and said, "Ling Chow..."

Debatable

The other day I was at my friend's home, and his tenth-grade son came into the kitchen. With his speech impediment, he told his dad, "I-I-I w-w-wa-want t-t-t-to try out f-f-fo-for the debate team."

His dad always supported him and believed in him—so

he told his son he thought he could do it. The next day the son came home from school dejected. His dad asked him if he made the debate team.

His son replied, "N-n-n-no. Th-th-th-they s-s- sa-said I w-w-wa-wasn't t-t-tall enough."

Honest Observation

One of my buddies told me he had two gay dads. I was like, "That's good bro. Because it would be weird if only one of them was gay!"

Karma

It turns out my older brother might need a kidney transplant. He should have probably thought about this possibility when I asked him if I could drive his cool car to the prom back in 1973!

Parenting 101

I got married and a part of me wanted kids, but a bigger part of me never wanted to do homework again! But I knew I would be an astute dad because although my parents never caught me smoking weed, it turns out they did know sober people don't give their parents good night handshakes! As a sports fan, I once attended a Yankees baseball game and thought there was no way I would ever pay $10 for a beer. But after I had my first daughter and eventually attended her first dance competition, after sitting through eight hours of relives and fouettés, I realized I would pay $100 for a beer!

Papa Bear Dad

Once when a young man pulled up in the driveway to take out my sister, my dad screamed, "You can't go out with him. He's driving a van!"

My mother asked, "Why not dear? You used to drive a van."

Frantically, my dad yelled back, "That's what I mean. You cannot go out with a guy who drives a van!"

Father Knows Best

Every time a young man knocked on our door to visit one of my three daughters, I always answered the door, invited him in, and pulled him aside to share my expectations. I would put my arm around him, look him in the eyes and explain, "We don't have a lot of rules around here. But the entire time you are with my daughter and out of my sight, I want you to whistle and clap. Because if I know where your lips and hands are at all times, you can stay here until Thursday!"

Innocence

A three-year-old found his dad's military identification tag and asked his mother what it was. His mother replied, "It's your father's dog tag."

The child then asked, "When was Daddy a dog?"

Nursery

The same three-year-old gained an interesting perspective on birth. His mother was pregnant, and so was the family dog. So, the mother thought it would be a good time to explain where babies come from. The boy stood wide-eyed and watched the birth of the puppies. Months later, on the day of delivery, the same child went to the hospital to visit his mother. As he looked at the row of babies through the nursery window, he asked, "Are these all ours?"

Perspective

Another three-year-old put his shoes on by himself. His mother noticed that the left shoe was on the right foot. She said, "Son, your shoes are on the wrong feet."

He looked up at her with a raised brow and said, "Don't kid me, Mom. They're the only feet I got!"

As A Child

We were eating one evening when my five-year-old daughter stood on her chair and reached for the bread. Attempting to teach her some etiquette, I said, "Why don't you sit down and ask your brother to pass it?"

She sweetly replied, "Okay, Daddy." Then she yelled across the table, "Give me the bread!"

"What's the magic word?" I asked.

"Now!" she replied.

School

On the first day of school, the kindergarten teacher said, "If anyone has to go to the bathroom, hold up two fingers."

This same five-year-old girl asked, "How will that help?"

Generational Laughs

One day, a little girl was talking to her mother and noticed that she had several strands of white hair on her head. She asked, "Why are a few of your hairs white, Mommy?"

Her mother replied, "Well, every time you are a bad girl and do something wrong, one of my hairs turns white."

The little girl responded, "Mommy, how come all of Grandma's hairs are white?"

Pure-Hearted Worship

A mother took her three-year-old daughter to church for the first time. Suddenly, the church lights dimmed as the choir walked down the aisle carrying lighted candles. All was quiet until the little girl started to sing in a loud voice, "Happy birthday to you, happy birthday to you..."

Moral Lesson

A mother was preparing pancakes for her sons, Kevin (five) and Ryan (three). The boys began to argue over who would get the first pancake. Their mother saw the opportunity for a moral lesson. "If Jesus were sitting here, He would say, "Let my brother have the first pancake. I can wait." Kevin turned to his younger brother and said, "Good Ryan, you be Jesus."

Parenting

Parents have taken communication to another level. How many times have we heard our dear mother say things like, "Don't climb up that tree. If you fall down and break both your legs, then don't come running to me!"

Or, when we've been in an accident, how many times have we heard our mother's classic question, "Do you have on clean underwear?"

I have even observed parents spanking their sons and yelling, "Don't hit your sister!" and other parents reprimanding their daughters, "Why are you talking with your mouth full? Answer me!"

Naming Kids

The old rock-and-roll musician Frank Zappa had three children. His son's name is Dweezle. His oldest daughter's name is Moon Unit. Zappa's youngest daughter's name is Motorhead. What an idiot. Everybody knows Motorhead is a boy's name!

Game Warden

A couple of young boys were fishing at their special pond off the beaten track. All of a sudden, the Game Warden jumped out of the bushes. Immediately, one of the boys threw his rod down and started running through the woods like a bat out of hell. The Game Warden was hot on his heels. After about a half mile, the young man stopped and stooped over with his hands on his thighs to catch his breath, so the Game Warden finally caught up to him.

"Let's see yer fishin' license, Boy!" the Warden gasped.

With that, the boy pulled out his wallet and gave the Game Warden a valid fishing license. "Well, son," said the Game Warden. "You must be about as dumb as a box of rocks! You don't have to run from me if you have a valid license!"

"Yes, sir," replied the young guy. "But my friend back there didn't have one."

Heroes

My son came home from school in the seventh grade and told me they engaged in an interesting project on the significance of heroes. He hugged me and said he had chosen me as his hero. I teared up and asked why he chose me. He said, "Because I couldn't spell Arnold Schwartnegger!"

Happiness is not just in the destination, but in the journey.

It's not the sugar that makes the tea sweet—it's the stirring!

Dan Clark
AND ASSOCIATES

POLITICS

Coincidence?

The 'Wizard of Oz' movie is now over 86 years old. If Dorothy were to encounter men with no heart, no brains, and no courage, she wouldn't be in Oz. She would be in Washington DC!

Timeless Suspicions

I don't make political jokes. Too many of them get elected.

The reason Politicians try so hard to get re-elected is that they would hate to have to make a living under the laws they have passed.

I think Congressmen should wear uniforms like NASCAR drivers, so we could identify their corporate sponsors.

Wake Up America

Over five thousand years ago, Moses said to the children

of Israel, "Pick up your shovels, mount your asses and camels, and I will lead you to the Promised Land."

Over 75 years ago, (when Welfare was introduced) President Roosevelt said, "Lay down your shovels, sit on your asses, and light up a Camel, this is the Promised Land."

Today Congress has stolen our shovels, taxed our assess, raised the price of camels and mortgaged the Promised Land!

I was so depressed last night thinking about the economy, the wars, lost jobs, savings, Social Security, retirement funds, etc. I called a Suicide Hotline. I had to press 3 for English. I was connected to a call center in Afghanistan. And when I told them I was suicidal, they got excited and asked if I could drive a truck!

Politics

"Poli" is a Latin word meaning "many" and "tics" means "Bloodsucking creatures." If "con" is the opposite of "pro," is Congress the opposite of progress?

Taxes

A little girl wrote a letter to God, asking for $100 dollars so she could buy herself a bicycle. She addressed it simply to GOD and placed it in the mailbox.

When the postman saw the letter with no address, he decided to add the street number and zip code of the post office in Washington D.C. and sent it off. When a post office clerk in D.C. saw the letter addressed to God, he immediately opened it and read the little girl's note. Touched by her request, he put a $10 dollar bill in an envelope and mailed it back to her with the following reply: "Enclosed is $10 dollars to use towards buying your bicycle."

When the little girl received the letter, she excitedly opened it, read the note, and immediately wrote her response: "Dear God. Thanks for the ten dollars. But next time please don't send it through Washington D.C.. They kept $90 dollars!"

Hiring Practices

Once upon a time there was a king who wanted to go fishing. He called the royal weather forecaster and enquired as to the weather forecast for the next few hours. The weatherman assured him that there was no chance of rain in the coming days.

So, the king went fishing with his wife, the queen. On the way, he met a farmer on his donkey. Upon seeing the king, the farmer said: "Your Majesty, you should return to the palace at once because in just a short time I expect a huge amount of rain to fall in this area".

The king was polite and considerate and replied: "I hold the palace meteorologist in high regard. He is an extensively educated and experienced professional. Besides, I pay him very high wages. He gave me a very different forecast. I trust him and I will continue on my way." So, he continued on his way.

However, a short time later a torrential rain fell from the sky. The King and Queen were totally soaked and their entourage worried upon seeing them in such a shameful condition.

Furious, the king returned to the palace and gave the order to fire the weatherman at once! Then he summoned the farmer and offered him the prestigious and high paying role of royal forecaster.

The farmer said: "Your Majesty, I do not know anything about forecasting. I obtain my information from my donkey. If I see my donkey's ears drooping, it means with certainty that it will rain."

So, the king hired the donkey. And so began the practice of hiring Asses to work in the government and occupy its highest and most influential positions.

President Bush And Moses

President Bush and his secret service are walking

through a building when they see an old man with a beard and walking stick, wearing a robe and sandals. President Bush immediately sends over one of his men to speak to the man. "Excuse me, President Bush wants to know if you're Moses?" The old man lowers his head and doesn't say a word.

Again, the agent asks, "Sir, the president wants to know if you are Moses?" Again, the old man says nothing. Frustrated, President Bush walks over himself and asks, "Are you Moses?" This time, the old man turns his back and walks away. President Bush and his entourage storm off.

Seeing what happened, a curious bystander approaches the old man and asks the same question, "Are you Moses?" This time the old man answers, "Yes, I am." The bystander asks, "Then why didn't you acknowledge that to the president?"

Moses answers, "Because the last time I talked to a bush, I ended up wandering in the wilderness for forty years and leading my people to the only place in the Middle East that doesn't have any oil!"

Partisan Politics

The way to eliminate partisan politics is to combine the strengths and truths of both the Republicans and the Democrats into one new super "after-hours party" called either the "Republocrats" or the "Demolicans." In this way we can solve all of America's problems with just a little compromise. For example, most Republicans believe in "pro life" but at the same time believe in "execution," while most Democrats believe in the women's "right to choose" but they never choose the "death penalty." Bottom line?

Both parties have the same fundamental belief in murder, but they just can't agree on the timing! So, let's not call it "abortion," let's call it "premature law enforcement," and don't call it an "execution" - call it a "termination in the ninety-fourth trimester!"

Republican or Democrat?

A man in a hot air balloon realized he was lost. He reduced altitude and spotted a woman below. He descended a bit more and shouted, "Excuse me, can you help me? I promised a friend I would meet him an hour ago, but I don't know where I am."

The woman replied, "You are in a hot air balloon approximately thirty feet above the ground. You are between forty- and forty-one-degrees north latitude and between fifty-nine- and sixty-degrees west longitude."

"You must be a republican," said the balloonist.

"I am," replied the woman.

"How did you know?"

"Well," answered the balloonist, "Everything you told me is technically correct, but I have no idea what to make of your information, and the fact is I am still lost. Frankly, you have not been much help so far."

The woman below responded. "You must be a democrat."

"I am," replied the balloonist, "but how did you know?"

"Well," said the woman, "You don't know where you are or where you are going. You have risen to where you are due to a large quantity of hot air. You made a promise, which you have no idea how to keep, and you expect me to solve your problem. The fact is—you are in exactly the same position you were in before we met, but now, somehow, it's all my fault."

Money

A Republican and a Democrat were walking down the street when they came to a homeless person. The Republican gave him his business card and told him to stop by for a job. He then took $20 out of his pocket and handed it to him.

The Democrat was impressed, and when they came to another homeless person, he decided it was his turn to help. So, he reached into the Republican's pocket and gave the man $50.

Government Employment

The government has a vast scrap yard in the middle of the desert. The congressman whose district it's in says someone might steal from it at night, so Congress creates a night watchman, GS-4 position and hires a person for the job. Then the congressman asks, "How does the watchman do his job without instruction?"

So, Congress creates a planning position and hires two people - one person to write the instructions, a GS-12, and one person to do time studies, a GS-11.

"How will we know the night watchman is doing the tasks correctly?" the Congressman asks.

So, Congress creates a quality control position and hires a GS-9 to do quality control studies and a GS-11 to write the reports. Then the Congressman asks, "How are these people going to get paid?"

So, Congress authorizes a position of timekeeper, GS-9, and payroll officer, GS-11, and two people are hired to fill the slots.

"Who will be accountable for all of these people?" the Congressman asks.

So, they hire three people, and administrative officer,

GS-13, an assistant administrative officer GS-12, and a legal secretary, a GS-8. On the eve of the next election season, the Congressman looks at the cost and says, "We have had this command in operation for one year and we are $40,000 over budget. We must cut back overall costs." So, they laid off the night watchman.

Government Bailout

Three contractors are bidding to fix a broken fence at the White House. One is from Chicago, another is from Tennessee, and the third is from Minnesota. All three go with a White House official to examine the fence. The Minnesota contractor takes out a tape measure and does some measuring, then works some figures with a pencil. "Well," he says, "I figure the job will run about $900. $400 for materials, $400 for my crew, and $100 profit for me."

The Tennessee contractor also does some measuring and figuring, then says, "I can do this job for $700. $300 for materials, $300 for my crew, and $100 profit for me." The Chicago contractor doesn't measure or figure, but leans over to the White House official and whispers, "$2,700."

The official, incredulous, says, "You didn't even measure like the other guys! How did you come up with such a high figure?" The Chicago contractor whispers back,

"$1000 for me, $1000 for you, and we hire the guy from Tennessee to fix the fence," "Done!" replies the government official.

And that, my friends, is how the new stimulus plan will work.

Famous Political Truths

Thomas Jefferson said, "A government big enough to give you everything you want is strong enough to take everything you have."

Winston Churchill said, "If you're not a liberal at age twenty, you have no heart. If you're not a conservative at age forty, you have no brain."

Ronald Reagan said, "I contend that for a nation to try to tax itself into prosperity is like a man standing in a bucket and trying to lift himself up by the handle."

Will Rogers said, "I don't make jokes. I just watch the government and report the facts."

Mark Twain said, "If you don't read the newspaper, you are uninformed. If you do read the newspaper, you are misinformed."

Tragic Truths

"We hang the petty thieves and appoint the great ones to public office."

"In my many years I have come to a conclusion that one useless man is a shame, two is a law firm, and three or more is a Congress."

"Talk is cheap, except when Congress does it."

"Suppose you were an idiot. And suppose you were a member of Congress. But then I repeat myself."

"No man's life, liberty, or property is safe while the legislature is in session."

"The only difference between a taxman and a taxidermist is that the taxidermist leaves the skin."

"There is no distinctly Native American criminal class, save Congress."

"The inherent vice of capitalism is the unequal sharing of the blessings. The inherent blessing of socialism is the equal sharing of misery."

"'A government which robs Peter to pay Paul can always depend on the support of Paul."

"'A liberal is someone who feels a great debt to his fellow man, which debt he proposes to pay off with your money."

"Foreign aid might be defined as a transfer of money from poor people in rich countries to rich people in poor countries."

"Government is the great fiction, through which

everybody endeavors to live at the expense of everybody else."

"Government's view of the economy could be summed up in a few short phrases: If it moves, tax it. If it keeps moving, regulate it. And if it stops moving, subsidize it."

"If you think health care is expensive now, wait until you see what it costs when it's free!"

"Just because you do not take an interest in politics doesn't mean politics won't take an interest in you!"

"What this country needs are more unemployed politicians."

A Billion

The next time you hear a politician use the word "billion" casually think about whether you do, or don't, want that politician spending your tax money.

A billion is a difficult number to comprehend, but an advertising agency did a good job of putting that figure in perspective for us all in one of its releases:

A billion seconds ago, it was 1959. A billion minutes ago, Jesus was alive.

A billion hours ago, our ancestors were living in the Stone Age.

A billion dollars ago, was only 8 hours and 20 minutes at

the rate Washington spends our money.

Unbelievably Amusing

In an interview, former Vice President Dan Quail asked former Russian President Mikhail Gorbachev, "What's that red thing on your forehead?" Gorby answered, "It's a birthmark." Quail asked, "How long have you had that?"

Former Vice President Al Gore screwed up twice in the same week when he said, "It's wonderful to be here in the great state of Chicago." Gore then said, "I was recently on a tour of Latin America, and the only regret I have was that I didn't study Latin harder in school so I could talk to those people."

Bill Clinton is getting twelve million dollars for his memoirs, and Hillary got eight million dollars for hers. That's twenty million dollars for two people who, for eight years, repeatedly testified that they couldn't remember anything - and now can't even remember emails from the Saturday before last!

Let's face it. Every country has its share of pompous windbag leaders who think they are better than everyone else. Ever since I visited the American cemetery in Normandy and saw the thousands of crosses of the American soldiers who died defending France and restoring her freedom, I snap every time a

Frenchman bad-mouths America, sand remember my high school days when my parents encouraged me to get more culture. So, I joined the French Club. It wasn't anything like they promised. The highlight of the year was when the French Club surrendered to the German Club twice without even a fight!

Clocks in Heaven

A man died and went to heaven. As he stood in front of St. Peter at the pearly gates he saw a huge wall of clocks. He asked, "What are the clocks? St. Peter explained they are 'Lie-Clocks.' Everyone on earth has a clock. Every time you lie the hands on your clock will move."

"Oh," said the man. "Whose clock is that?"

"It's Mother Theresa's. The hands have never moved. Indicating she had never told a lie."

"And whose is that clock?" pointing at the wall.

"St. Peter replied, "That's Abraham Lincoln's clock. The hands have moved twice. Indicating he had told only two lies his entire life."

The man then asked, "Where is Joe Biden's clock?" St. Peter smiled, "It's in Jesus's office. He is using it as a ceiling fan!"

A broken clock
is right twice a day.

Never give up
on anyone —
especially yourself!
Make peace with
what you're not!

ITS ONE O'CLOCK...

...ON THE DOT!

LESSONS IN HUMOR

Out of the Mouth of Babes

When my daughter was six years old and we pulled into the shopping mall parking lot, she looked out the window and then looked at me and asked, "When are they going to pass a law so handicapped people can park wherever they want?" (Think about it until you get it!)

Everything I Needed to Know I Learned From Blain

In-the-box right answers present a challenge. Too often the learned discount them because they are simple and ordinary enough for the unlearned to understand. For some reason, we think that unless an answer is complicated, it isn't sophisticated, and if it's obvious, it can't be life-altering or an educational experience worth our while. Well, well, well. Apparently, they have never met anybody like my big buddy Blain!

He was my first roommate at the university - a big,

strong, soft-spoken cowboy, with a huge smile, who was always polite and did not speak much. When we met, I asked, "What's your name?"

"Blain," he answered.

Five minutes of silence later, I asked, "Where are you from?"

"Idaho."

Five minutes of silence later, I asked, "Do you live in the city or the country?"

"Country."

Five minutes of silence later, I asked, "What is your major?"

He said, "Communications."

Ha!

Yes, Blain was a man of few words, but when he did speak, he was always deep and profound. In our first seven days together, Blain taught me everything I needed to know to succeed for the rest of my life.

Day One: We were late checking into our dorm room, so we got last pick of the accommodations. We were told that the only thing left was an older corner room. I complained all the way down the hall, moaning, "I never get a break." Then we opened the door and saw a big, oak-trimmed suite. Blain quietly said, "The early bird gets the worm, but the second mouse always gets the cheese."

Day Two: I had an old car with squeaky brakes. I asked Blain if he knew anything about cars. He said, "I'll see." That afternoon he jacked up my car and took off a wheel. He quickly checked it and put it back on. He then opened the hood and fiddled around for a minute. Dumbfounded, I asked him what he was doing? He simply replied, "I couldn't fix your brakes, so I just made your horn louder!"

Day Three: We had the first class of the day together. It was Introduction to Marketing. The professor said, "Take thirty minutes and write an ad. Use as many words as necessary, but keep it to one page." After a while, the professor called on three different people to share. They read full-page, wordy essays. The professor then called on Blain.

He quietly read, "For sale: Parachute, only used once, never opened, small stain." We laughed. The professor was intrigued and inquired if he had any other thoughts he would like to share. Blain quietly drawled, "Well I kinda, sorta got a real-estate marketing idea I also wrote here."

The professor said, "Yes?" as we all held our breath.

Blain read, "Statistics prove that most people have serious accidents within five miles of their home. So, call me as your realtor, and I'll help you move!" We all burst into belly-shaking hoots and cheers!

Day Four: The sociology professor ironically didn't seem to care about anything or anyone. He didn't call the roll and only talked for one minute at the beginning of class to tell us what chapters to read. Then he sat down, put his feet up on a table, and read a magazine for the next thirty minutes. I commented to Blain, "How can he teach us when he is not even involved in the class?"

"He can't," Blain replied. "You can't farm from the city." I then asked him if he were the professor, what would he teach?

Blain replied, "Ninety percent of success is half mental."

I laughed and asked, "What?"

With a serious face, Blain explained: "Yep. Success is 10 percent inspiration and 90 percent perspiration—10 percent what happens to you and 90 percent what you do with what happens to you. The half mental is attitude and the other half is action."

Day Five: Already, some of the guys in our dorm had started to party during the week with their wild roommates. I commented, "Mike came in here straight, with high moral standards and high athletic and education goals, but John sure is a bad influence on him."

Blain replied, "Yep. I had to write poetry in English class today and wouldn't you know it, it pretty much explains what's goin' on with these fellas: "I wrote: On top of old Smokey all covered with snow, I lost my best bird dog by aiming too low. It's better to shoot for the stars and miss than to aim for a pile of manure and hit!"

I hadn't seen Blain talk this much all at once since I met him, and I definitely didn't want to cut him off. I'm glad I didn't because he then shared this poem:

With garbage and junk our big can is well fed

This trash we don't want we can burn it instead

But what about dirt that you've heard or said,

Oh what can be done with a garbage can head?

Day Six: It was the weekend, and I asked Blain if he wanted to go to a party. We went. Within fifteen minutes the fraternity boys tried to pressure him with the usual, "C'mon. Chill out. Loosen up. Smoke a little dope, drink a few shots, get down tonight." I asked him if he wanted to leave. Blain answered, "No." But they shouldn't try to teach a pig to sing. It's a waste of your time, and it annoys the pig! Why should I let what others say and do change who I am or what I do?"

Day Seven: I was tired and wanted to sleep in. But Blain was up bright and early. I asked him where he was going all dressed up. He said, "Church."

Sarcastically, I poked fun. "Why would you go to church? Your parents aren't here to make you."

Blain put me in my place with his answer: "It's what you do when the coach is not around that makes you a champion. The Native American Indians say, 'Short alive, long time dead.' We shouldn't just learn and do things that will help us while we're alive; we should learn and do things that will help us when we are dead! You should come to church with me."

I defiantly demanded, "Give me one good reason why I should."

Blain pretty much summed up the week and the previous in-the-box principles of success he had already taught me when he answered, "It's better to build a fence at the edge of the cliff than to park an ambulance at its base!"

Look For Laughs

I believe there is truth in all humor and some humor in all truth. For example, if you feel sluggish and overweight and look at yourself in the mirror as a fat failure, is that positive or negative? Obviously, it destructively destroys your self-worth, dilutes your desire, and sabotages your belief that you can change. What if instead of seeing yourself as a fat failure, you saw yourself as someone who has been very successful at putting on weight? Ha! And with a positive attitude you now realize that because you gained one pound at a time, you can also lose one pound at a time.

A Stanford University study revealed that children laugh about three hundred times a day. Adults only laugh seventeen times a day. I guess that's why children live longer than adults! The study showed that 84 percent of executives believe that people with a sense of humor do a better job than those without one. People who frequently laugh, experience a lower risk of heart attack, stroke, hypertension, and depression.

Children don't have these problems. They set up lemonade stands and sell drinks in the hot sun. They invent things like an electric hot dog polisher and take the hair balls the cat coughed up to school for show and tell!

Dyslexia

Just found out why my buddy was never religious and didn't believe in God. He is dyslexic and it was difficult for him to worship "Dog!"'

Dog Lessons

- A dog is "Man's Best Friend" because Dogs Never Lie About Love and teach us to be loyal.

- When loved ones come home, they always run to greet them.

- When it's in their best interest, they practice obedience.

- Take naps and stretch before rising.

- Run, romp, and play daily.

- Never pretend to be something they're not.

- Avoid biting when a simple growl will do.

- No matter how often they're scolded, they don't buy into the guilt thing and pout... and run right back and make friends.

- Delight in the simple joy of a long walks, and never pass up a joyride to bask in a sunny day with the wind in their face.

Company Laughs

There is a Fortune 100 company where the leaders meet once a month to brainstorm and discuss products and services. When they enter the boardroom, they each put on a large, brightly colored Hawaiian shirt. The CEO puts on Mickey Mouse ears. Immediately, they have permission to think outside the lines and let their imaginations run wild! As a result, the ideas flow more freely and the meetings have more than tripled their productivity. Bottom line? The leaders live by five beliefs:

- If you can't be funny, be fun!

- Establish a humor network by inviting people to relax and laugh around you.

- Leave a Slinky or Rubik's Cube on your desk for people

to play with while talking to you.

- Always take your job seriously – Never take yourself serious!

- Always look and listen for the humorous, odd and amusing things that people say and do around you so they trigger your endorphins, alter your attitude, turn your frown upside down, and make you go 'Huh?'

Getting Out of a Ticket

A woman gets pulled over for speeding. Woman: Is there a problem, Officer? Officer: Ma'am, you were speeding. Woman: Oh, I see. Officer: Can I see your driver's license please? Woman: I'd give it to you, but I don't have one. Officer: Don't have one? Woman: I lost it four years ago for drunk driving. Officer: Oh. Then may I see your vehicle registration papers, please? Woman: Can't do that either. Officer: Why not? Older Woman: I stole this car. Officer: Stole it? Woman: Yes, and I kidnapped the owner, tied him up, and stuffed him in the trunk, if you want to take a look. The Officer looks at the woman, slowly backs away, and calls for back-up.

Within minutes, five police cars roar up to the site. A senior officer slowly steps out of his car and approaches the woman, clasping his gun in both hands.

Officer 2: Ma'am, could you step out of your vehicle, please? The woman steps out of her vehicle. Woman: Is there a problem, sir? Officer 2: One of my officers told me that you have stolen this car and kidnapped the owner. Woman: Kidnapped the owner? Officer 2: Yes, could you open the trunk of your car, please? The woman opens the trunk, revealing nothing but an empty trunk. Officer 2: Is this your car, ma'am? Woman: Yes, here are the registration papers.

Officer 2 is stunned: One of my officers claims that you don't have a driver's license. The woman digs into her handbag, pulls out a license, and hands it to the officer, who examines it. He looks puzzled. Officer 2: Thank you, ma'am. One of my officers told me you didn't have a license, that you stole this car, and that you kidnapped and tied up the owner.

Woman: I bet the lying SOB told you I was speeding, too!

Pavlov

Pavlov is sitting in a pub enjoying a pint, when the phone rings and he jumps up shouting, "Crap, I forgot to feed the dog!"

Idiots At Work

I was signing the receipt for my credit card purchase

when the clerk noticed that I had never signed my name on the back of the credit card. She informed me that she could not complete the transaction unless the card was signed. When I asked why, she explained that it was necessary to compare the signature on the credit card with the signature I just signed on the receipt. So, I signed the credit card in front of her. She carefully compared that signature to the one I signed on the receipt. As luck would have it, they matched!

Alcohol

I just read that drinking is bad for you, so I stopped reading!

People say that drinking milk makes you stronger. Yet, when you drink five glasses of milk and try to move a wall? You can't. However, if you drink five glasses of wine the wall moves itself!

Wine Pairing In the Stone Age: Simple rule of thumb: 'If it tries to eat us, serve with red. If it runs away from us, serve with white.'

Idiots On the Highway

A truck driver was driving along on the freeway. A sign suddenly appeared: Low Bridge. Before he could stop, he hit it and got stuck. Cars were backed up for miles. Finally, a police car arrived. The cop got out of his car and walked around to the truck driver, put his hands on his hips, and said, "Got stuck, huh?"

The truck driver said, "No, I was delivering this bridge and ran out of gas."

Idiots In Service

Last time I had a flat tire, I pulled my truck into one of those side-of-the-road gas stations. The attendant walked out, looked at my truck, looked at me, and said, "Tahr go flat?"

I said, "Nope. I was driving around and those other three just swelled right up on me."

Idiots In the Neighborhood

I live in a semi-rural area. We recently had a new neighbor call the local township administrative office to request the removal of the Deer Crossing sign on our road. The reason: Many deer were being hit by cars, and she no longer wanted them to cross there.

Forrest Gump

Forrest died, met St. Peter at the gates, who explained he needed to answer three questions to get into heaven. "How many days of the week start with the letter "T?" Forrest answered, "Two - Today and Tomorrow." St. Peter rubbed his head and said, "That's not the answer we were going for, but we're going to give it to you!"

"The next question is, how many seconds are in a year?" Forrest answered, "12. There is January 2nd, February 2nd..."

"And the last question is, what is another name for God?" "That's easy!" Forrest replied. Andy!"

"Where did you learn that?" Peter inquired. "In the song - Andy walks with me, Andy talks with me..."

Supply

Being a high school Principal isn't so bad because you get a lifetime supply of toilet paper if you're just willing to climb up into the trees every weekend and get it.

Choosing Words Wisely

On a British version of the TV Game Show "Family Feud," the Host asked a contestant some provocative questions trying to solicit risqué answers to get higher ratings. What happened was more entertaining than the expected! The first Question: What does a cow have four of that a woman only has two of? Contestant: Legs.

Question: What is in a man's pants that is not in a woman's pants? Contestant: Pockets.

Question: What does a man do standing up, a woman do sitting down, and a dog does on three legs? Contestant: Shake Hands.

Question: What does a dog do that man steps into? Contestant: Pants.

Frustrated, the Host asked: What word starts with 'F' and ends with a 'K' that means a lot of heat and excitement? Contestant: Fire Truck.

Tornado Season

Tornado tip of the day: Keep a hot dog in your pocket. This way, the search dog will find you first!

Online Dating

I'll never join one of those 'Online Dating Services.' I prefer to meet someone the old-fashioned way through alcohol and poor judgement.

You can if you think you can!

When your attitude is right, your abilities will always catch up.

Dan Clark
AND ASSOCIATES

SERIOUS OBSERVATIONS

A recent police study found that you're much more likely to get shot by a fat cop if you run.

I went to a bookstore and asked the saleswoman where the Self-Help section was. She said if she told me, it would defeat the purpose.

You've got bad eating habits if you use a grocery cart in 7-Eleven!

Guilt is the reason they put articles in Playboy Magazine.

Most people work just hard enough not to get fired and get paid just enough money not to quit.

A house is just a place to keep your stuff while you go out and get more stuff.

Some people have no idea what they're doing, and a lot of them are really good at it.

Never argue with an idiot. They will only bring you down to their level and beat you with experience.

Ever wonder about those people who spend $5 apiece

on those little bottles of Evian water? Try spelling Evian backward (naïve).

Think of how stupid the average person is, and realize half of them are stupider than that.

Trying to be happy by accumulating possessions is like trying to satisfy hunger by taping sandwiches all over your body.

I bet you anything that 10 times out of 10, Nicky, Vinny and Tony will beat the s**t out of Todd, Kyle and Tucker.

Isn't making a smoking section in a restaurant like making a peeing section in a swimming pool.

If "Plan A" fails remember that you still have 25 other letters left.

Never get into fights with ugly people; they have nothing to lose.

If at first you don't succeed, skydiving is not for you.

I always wanted to be the last guy on earth, just to see if all these women were lying to me.

Have you noticed that everyone who is for abortion has already been born?

They call it the 24-Hour Flu because it compresses a week's worth of bathroom time into just one day!

When the stroke of midnight signifies that your car has just depreciated another $1000.

A pumpkin is nothing more than a Gourd with an incredible media campaign.

20 years ago, we had Johnny Cash, Bob Hope and Steve Jobs. Now we have no Cash, no Hope and no Jobs. Please don't let Kevin Bacon die!

Statistics

One day in my college human relations class the professor quoted a study by the Department of Motor Vehicles indicating that 23% of traffic accidents are alcohol related. He then asked what we could do to change this. My roommate Blain, raised his hand and commented, "This means that the remaining 77% of accidents are caused by dingbats who just drink coffee, carbonated drinks, juice, milk, water, and junk like that. Therefore, let us beware of those who do not drink alcohol, as they cause three times as many accidents!"

Names

I never realized the importance of names until the O.J. Simpson murder trial. I just heard that the Orange Juice Manufacturers of Florida offered O. J. twelve million dollars to change his name to Snapple!

What has 132 legs and eight teeth? The front row of a

Willie Nelson concert.

You know toothpaste was invented by a redneck. Otherwise, it would be called 'teethpaste.'

You Know You're A "Foxworthy Redneck" If...

Seventh grade is your senior year.

Your dad walks you to school because you're in the same grade.

You loved your summer job as a lifeguard until that blue guy got you fired.

You've never had to lug a paint can to the top of a water tower to defend your sister's honor.

Your wife's hairdo has ever been destroyed by a ceiling fan.

You go to your family reunion to pick up women.

Your richest relative buys a new house — and you have to help him take the wheels off it.

You think a six-pack and a bug zapper is quality entertainment.

Your family tree does not fork.

You've ever been too drunk to fish.

You've lost more than two teeth opening beer bottles.

You helped your cousin move his refrigerator -- and the

grass underneath it has turned yellow.

You know that in both a tornado and a redneck divorce someone is going to lose a trailer.

You go golfing, and a guy in your foursome gets the sports mixed up at the first tee, puts on his golf glove, and when a guy on the group ahead of you addresses his ball, he starts yelling, "Hey batter, batter - swing, batter, batter!"

Celebrities

In the movie 'Toy Story,' actor Tom Hanks played a cowboy. In 'Saving Private Ryan,' he played a soldier. In 'Cast Away,' he played a shirtless hairy dude. When he finally plays a Native American, he'll have achieved something called the 'Village People grand slam.'

After months of dating, Taylor Swift broke up with her boyfriend, Connor Kennedy. And when Kennedy asked if they were ever getting back together, Taylor just handed him an iPod and said, "Play track six."

Why...

Why isn't phonetics spelled phonetically?

Why are there Braille signs at the drive-through

windows at the bank?

If a deaf kid swears, does his mom wash his hands with soap?

What's another word for synonym?

Why do we drive on a parkway but park in a driveway?

Isn't it a bit unnerving that doctors call what they do "practice?"

Would a fly that loses its wings be called a "walk?"

If a turtle loses its shell is it naked or homeless?

If vegetarians eat vegetables, what do humanitarians eat?

If people can have triplets and quadruplets why not singlets and doublets?

Is Atheism a non-prophet organization?

If I went to a bookstore and asked the saleswoman, "Where is the self-help section?" She said that if she told me, it would defeat the purpose.

Why is "Abbreviated" such a long word?

Why is lemon juice made with artificial flavor and dishwashing liquid made with real lemons?

Why is the man who invests all your money called a broker?

Why is the time of day with the slowest traffic called rush hour?

Why are they called apartments when they are all stuck together?

If you blow in a dog's face he gets mad at you, but when you take him for a ride in a car he sticks his head out the window?

Why anyone going slower than you is an idiot, but anyone going faster is a maniac?

So... they can't locate non-documented, illegal aliens for deportation, but they can find them to give them money, food, free hotel rooms, and a cell phone paid for by U.S. tax paying citizens?!

Ever Wonder...

Why we say something is out of whack? What's a whack?

About Cheez Whiz? I know what cheese is, but what's whiz?

Why a wise man and a wise guy are opposites?

Why overlook and oversee have opposite meanings?

Why dolphins are so intelligent that within only a few weeks of captivity they can train Americans to stand at the very edge of the pool and throw them fish?

Why is it that if someone tells you there are 1 billion stars in the universe, you will believe them, but if they tell you that a wall has wet paint, you will have to touch it to be sure?

You Know You've Been in the Workplace Since The 1980's If...

A text was a book you checked out of the library.

Spam was inexpensive meat in a can.

A Tweet was something Barbara Walters gave to her pet dog.

You've sat at the same desk for four years and worked for three different companies.

Your company welcome sign was attached with Velcro.

Your resume is on a diskette in your pocket.

Your To Do List includes "go home."

Brave And Courageous

I was sitting in a restaurant when the man in the booth next to me asked what the special of the day was. The waitress replied, "Cow's tongue."

"Yuck" he said. "How could anyone eat anything that had been in something's mouth? I'll have two eggs."

As I laughed, he too realized the absurdity of his comments and we took the conversation further. "Can you imagine the first guy who ate an Egg?" I asked. Two old boys out on the farm. One says to the other, "Hey, the next thing that pops out of the south end of that chicken, I'll eat it. We'll call it an egg."

And what about the guys who drank milk for the first time. Same two old boys on the farm talking, "Hey, you yank on one of those long skinny hot dog looking things hanging down from under the back end of that cow and I'll drink whatever comes out. We'll call it milk."

And can you imagine the first guy who ate cheese? The same old boys accidentally leave a gallon of milk out in the corner of their hot kitchen. Two months later they discover it. One says to the other, "If you will scrape that green and black mold off of that block of hard curdled milk, I'll eat it. We'll call it cheese!"

America

It's the best place to sell something because we all want a great deal. We don't want to buy tires for $85 dollars, so they sell them to us for $39.95. Then we need to buy all the extras: "Do you want them on your car?" (No dummy, I just want to look at them!) $20 bucks per tire. "Do you want them balanced?" (No, I'm going to drive down the road bouncing!)

What Gender

Ziplock bags (Male): because they hold everything in, but you can always see right through them.

Swiss army knives (Male): because even though it appears useful for a wide variety of work, it spends most of its time just opening bottles.

Tire (Male): because it goes bald and often is over-inflated.

Subway car (Male): because it uses the same old lines to pick people up.

Remote control (Female - thought I'd say male): but It gives a man pleasure, he'd be lost without it, and while he doesn't always know the right buttons to push, he keeps trying!

Gender Flies

A man was walking around the kitchen with a fly swatter and his wife asked him what he was doing. He answered, "Hunting flies." She asked if he had killed any yet. He replied, "Yep. Three males and two females." She asked how he could tell them apart. Her husband replied, "Three were on a beer can and two were on the phone!"

Irony

The most shoplifted book in America is the Bible.

The founder of AA asked for whiskey on his deathbed.

Alexander Graham Bell invented the telephone but refused to keep one in his study. He feared it would distract him from his work.

The "Father of Traffic Safety" William Eno invented the stop sign, crosswalk, traffic circle, one-way street, and taxi stand – but never learned how to drive.

Q-tips, which are bought primarily to clean inside ears, are sold in boxes that expressly warn: "Do not insert inside the ear canal."

The only losing basketball coach in University of Kansas history is James Naismith – the man who invented basketball in 1891.

The first man to survive going over Niagara Falls in a barrel died after slipping on an orange peel.

Charlie Chaplin once entered a "Charlie Chaplin walk" contest... and came in 20th.

Al Capone's older brother was a Federal Prohibition Agent.

McDonald's own employee health page warns against eating McDonald's burgers and fries.

The condition of not being able to pronounce the letter R is called 'Rhotacism' (Yes you pronounce the R!)

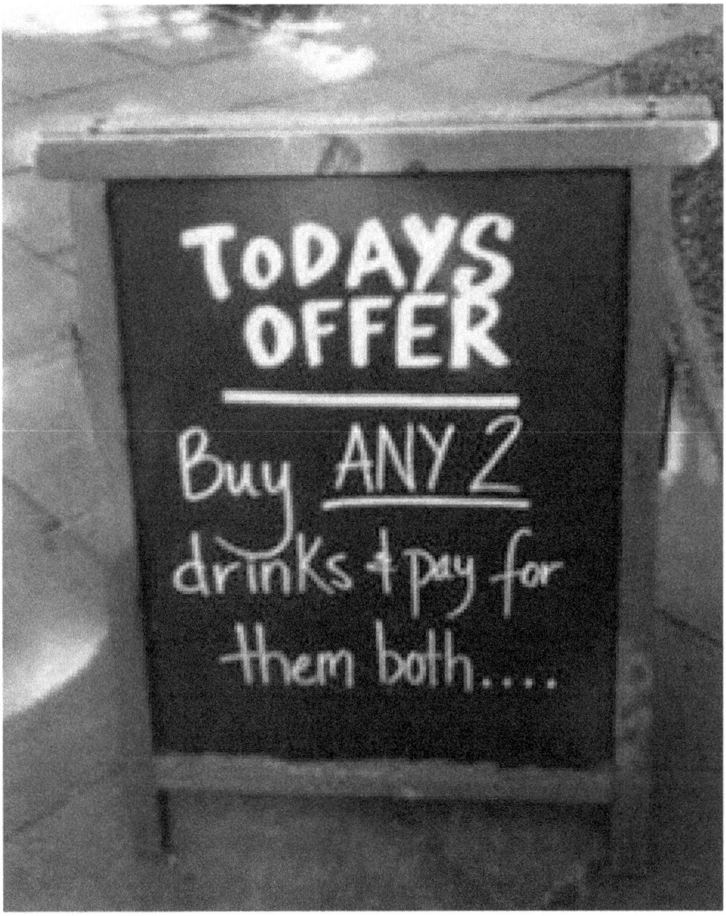
TODAYS OFFER
Buy ANY 2 drinks & pay for them both....

BEST OF EVERYTHING

Best Classified Ads

1 Man, 7 Woman Hot Tub—$850/or Best Offer

Butchering gloves: One 5-finger glove, one 3-finger glove. Pair: $15. Call Tuesday after I get my stitches out.

10 Cows—Never been bred. Also, 1 gay bull for sale—Best offer.

Nordic Track $300—hardly used. Call Chubbie.

Shakespeare's Pizza—Free chopsticks.

Best Comeback

Some Texans are mingling at the bar when a Harvard graduate walks in. "Howdy, stranger," one Texan says. "Where are you from?" The Harvard graduate answers, "I come from a place where we do not end our sentences in prepositions."

"Oh, I'm sorry," replies the Texan. "Where are you from, Jackass?"

Just changed my Facebook name to "No one" so when I

see stupid posts I can click 'Like' and it will say 'No one likes this.'

Best Headlines

Something Went Wrong in Jet Crash

Expert Says Man Steals Clock, Faces Time

Squad Helps Dog Bite Victim

Man Struck by Lightning, Faces Battery Charge

Killer Sentenced to Die for Second Time in 10 Years

Typhoon Rips Through Cemetery: Hundreds Dead

Hospitals Sued by Seven Foot Doctors

Best Country Song Titles

- May I buy you a drink so I look better?

- My Wife Ran Off With My Best Friend And I'm Going To Miss Him Dearly

- Had I Shot You When I Met You I'd Be Out Of Jail By Now

- Drink, drink, drink til you drink her pretty

- If The Phone Don't Ring, You'll Know It's Me

- How Can I Miss You If You Won't Go Away

- I'm So Miserable Without You; It's Like Having You Here

- She Got The Ring and I Got The Finger

-You're the Reason Our Kids Are So Ugly

- Ain't Never Gone To Bed With An Ugly Woman, But Sure Have Woke With a Few.

More Clever Signs

In a veterinarian's waiting room: "Be back in 5 minutes. Sit! Stay!"

On the maternity room door: "Push, Push, Push."

Outside a muffler shop: "No appointment necessary; we'll hear you coming."

In the front yard of a funeral home: "Drive carefully, we'll wait."

Door of a plastic surgeon's office: "We can help pick your nose."

At a tire shop in Milwaukee: "Invite us to your next blowout."

Sign at the psychic's employment hotline: "Don't call us, we'll call you."

In a counselor's office: "Growing old is mandatory, growing wise is optional."

A sign in a shoe repair store: "We will heel you. We will save your sole. We will even dye for you!"

Sign over a Gynecologist's Office: "Dr. George, at your cervix."

At an Eye Clinic: "If you don't see what you're looking for, you've come to the right place."

On a Plumber's truck: "We repair what your husband fixed."

On an Electrician's truck: "Let us remove your shorts."

In a Non-smoking Area: "If we see smoke, we will assume you are on fire and will take appropriate action."

At a Car Dealership: "The best way to get back on your feet - miss a car payment."

At the Electric Company: "We would be delighted if you send in your payment on time. However, if you don't, YOU will be de-lighted."

In a Restaurant window: "Don't stand there and be hungry; come on in and get fed up."

Sign on the back of a Septic Tank Truck: "Caution - This truck is full of Political Promises."

Best Quotes

"If at first you don't succeed... so much for skydiving." - Henny Youngman

"Researchers have discovered that chocolate produces some of the same reactions in the brain as marijuana. The researchers also discovered other similarities between the two, but they can't remember what they are." — Jimmy Falon on the Tonight Show.

"I asked God for a bike, but I know God doesn't work that way. So, I stole a bike and asked for forgiveness." — Emo Philips

"When I die, I want to go peacefully like my grandfather did – in his sleep. Not yelling and screaming like the passengers in his car." — Bob Monkhouse

"I intend to live forever. So far, so good." —Steven Wright

Honolulu - it's got everything. Sand for the children, sun for the wife, sharks for the wife's mother." — Ken Dodd

Best Customer Relations

I was eating at an all-you-can-eat Chinese buffet restaurant with three guys I used to play football with. Each of them still weighed about three hundred pounds. After our fourth trip through the line, the sweet little Asian manager came out and scolded us, "You been here fo owa! You big fat guys go now! You ee too much foo. I go bro!"

Best Answering Machine Messages

A is for academics. B is for beer. One of those reasons is why I'm not here.

Hi, this is Dan. If you are the phone company, I already sent the money. If you are my parents, please send money. If you are my financial institution, you didn't lend me enough money. If you are my friend, you owe me money. If you are female, don't worry, I have plenty of money. If you are a solicitor, I don't need light bulbs, my carpets cleaned, or my picture taken. I gave to charity at the office, and I am happy with my phone service.

"You've reached the cell phone of Dan Clark. I'm sorry I'm IN right now. If you please leave a message, I will call you when I'm OUT again."

MILITARY

Surprise

I'm not a member of the Air Force, but I've had some incredible flying experiences. I've done barrel rolls in Air Force One, shot down a Russian MIG, and would've landed the Space Shuttle if my kid's Xbox didn't crap out.

Military Observations

If the enemy is in range, so are you. — Infantry Journal

It is generally inadvisable to eject directly over the area you just bombed. — Air Force Manual

Whoever said the pen is mightier than the sword obviously never encountered automatic weapons. — General MacArthur

Tracers work both ways. — U.S. Army Ordinance

If you see a bomb technician running, keep up with him. — USAF Ammo Troop Manual

When one engine fails on a twin-engine airplane you always have enough power left to get you to the scene of the crash.

As the test pilot climbs out of the experimental aircraft, having torn off the wings and tail in the crash landing, the crash truck arrives. The rescuer sees a bloodied pilot and asks, "What happened?" The pilot replied: "I don't know, I just got here myself!" — (Lockheed test pilot)

Fighter Jet Fun

The first time I got a ride in a military fighter jet was at Pax River, Maryland. Should have turned around and gone back home as soon as I saw the welcome sign: "Home of the Naval Test Pilot School." Of course I had seen the awesome movie, "Top Gun," and of course I thought I was as much of a stud muffin hunk of burnin love as Tom Cruise was; so of course I pulled into the parking lot of the commanding officer and proceeded to strut my stuff up the stairs and into his office. After Marine Colonel "Gator" Thompson greeted me, we headed to breakfast.

I was confident I would see Kelly McGillis in the men's room and would be fitted with a flight suit that said Maverick. Neither happened. As we began breakfast, I asked the Colonel if there was something specific he thought I should eat before I flew the next morning. He said, "Yes, bananas." When I asked "why?" he smiled and explained, "Because they taste exactly the same coming up as they do going down!"

After breakfast I went for my flight physical where the doctor examined things I didn't even have. Then off to see the F-18 I was going to fly, which led to the first part of my intense preparation - "Spatial Disorientation Training," where a scowling Lieutenant - call sign "Psycho," strapped me onto an exotic bar stool, spun me around for fifteen minutes as if I had lost control of the plane and needed to regain my equilibrium, and then asked me to walk to the door and turn on the light. Ha! I felt like I was at a bad fraternity party!

Yes, I nearly drowned when I had to dive into an Olympic sized swimming pool in eighty-five pounds of combat gear and swim two lengths, with the trainer smiling hoping I wouldn't survive.

Yes, they strapped me to a sled and shot me up a hundred feet several times to simulate ejecting from a plane. And yes, they fitted me in a parachute harness and hung me from a high bar for ten minutes, which was supposed to simulate gliding in a chute to earth, but actually felt like someone kicked me in the groin, and then had to jump off a ten-foot-high wall and tuck and roll several times to simulate landing. Not funny at all.

Finally, morning came, and I was again outfitted in my flight gear and introduced to my pilot. No, his call sign was not "Maverick" or "Iceman" or "Cougar." His name was Bill Rooter - call sign "Roto." That's right. I was flying with and putting my life in the hands of "Roto Rooter!"

Again, not funny!

We flew for 90 minutes, soared to 45,000 feet altitude to dive bomb straight down (as if we weren't going fast enough!), catching 7.5 Gs, going Mach 2, engaging in aileron rolls, loops, and flying in formation with another F-18. and simulated bombing runs.

When we finally landed and I put my nose and mouth back in the middle of my face where they belonged, I felt like I was having labor pains, and that someone had been grabbing my bottom lip and pulling it up over my head for the last hour!

Bottom line? Of course I popped my cookies! Colonel Thompson was right about the bananas. In fact, I also ejected some pizza from three nights before, and a box of Milk Duds I had eaten at a movie when I was nine! Holy flippin cow! I was upside down for so long I think I am the only human being who has ever "thrown down!" And when it came time for my "Call Sign" ceremony I was praying they wouldn't name me 'Two Bags!'

As I climbed down the ladder and waddled over to thank the Colonel for this exhilarating experience, I didn't know if I should curse him for feeling like someone had grabbed my bottom lip and pulled it up over my head, or thank him for having lost twenty pounds in water weight, and getting liposuction, a facelift, tummy tuck, and a 1200 mile-an-hour enema for free!

Signal

Through the pitch-black night, the captain sees a light dead ahead on a collision course with his ship. He sends a signal: "Change your course ten degrees east." The light signals back: "Change yours, ten degrees west." Angry, the captain sends: "I'm a Navy captain! Change your course, sir!" "I'm a seaman, second class," comes the reply. "Change your course, sir."

"Now the captain is furious. "I'm a battleship! I'm not changing course!" There is one last reply. "I'm a lighthouse. Your call."

Beneficiary

Airman Jones was assigned to the induction center, where he advised new recruits about their government benefits, especially their GI insurance. It wasn't long before Captain Smith noticed that Airman Jones was having a staggeringly high success-rate, selling insurance to nearly 100% of the recruits he advised. Rather than ask about this, the Captain stood in the back of the room and listened to Jones' sales pitch.

Jones explained the basics of the GI Insurance to the new recruits and then said: "If you have GI Insurance and go into battle and are killed, the government has to pay

$200,000 to your beneficiaries. If you don't have GI insurance, and you go into battle and get killed, the government only has to pay a maximum of $6000. Now," he concluded, "which group do you think they are going to send into battle first?"

Slap!

A young Marine and his commanding officer board a train headed through the mountains of Switzerland. They can find no place to sit except for two seats right across the aisle from a young woman and her grandmother.

After a while, it is obvious that the young woman and the young soldier are interested in each other because they are giving each other "looks."

Soon the train passes into a tunnel and it is pitch black. There is a sound of the smack of a kiss followed by the sound of the smack of a slap. When the train emerges from the tunnel, the four sit there without saying a word. The grandmother is thinking to herself: "It was very brash for that young soldier to kiss my granddaughter, but I'm glad she slapped him."

The commanding officer is sitting there thinking, "I didn't know the young Marine was brave enough to kiss the girl, but I sure wish she hadn't missed him when she slapped and hit me!"

The young woman was sitting and thinking: "I'm glad the soldier kissed me, but I wish my grandmother had not slapped him!"

The young Marine sat there with a satisfied smile on his face. He thought to himself. "Life is good. When does a fellow have the chance to kiss a beautiful girl and slap his commanding officer all at the same time!"

Photo

The soldier serving in Hong Kong was annoyed and upset when his girl wrote breaking off their engagement and asking for her photograph back. He went out and collected from his friends all the unwanted photographs of women that he could find, bundled them all together and sent them back with a note saying, "I regret to inform you that I cannot remember which one is you — please keep your photo and return the others."

The Private

It was a dark, stormy night. The Marine was on his first assignment, and it was guard duty.

A General stepped out taking his dog for a walk. The nervous young Private snapped to attention, made a perfect salute, and snapped out "Sir, Good Evening, Sir!"

The General, out for some relaxation, returned the salute and said, "Good evening soldier, nice night, isn't it?"

Although it was raining, the Private wasn't going to disagree with the General, so he saluted again and replied, "Sir, yes Sir!"

The General continued, "You know there's something about a stormy night that I find soothing and relaxing. Don't you agree?"

The Private didn't agree, but because he was just a Private he responded, "Sir, yes, sir!"

The General, pointing at the dog, then said, "This is a Golden Retriever, the best type of dog to train. I got this dog for my wife."

The Private simply replied, "Good trade Sir!"

Camo

The Sergeant Major growled at the young soldier, "I didn't see you at camouflage training this morning." "Thank you very much, sir."

Sex

A U.S. Marine Colonel was about to start the morning briefing to his staff. While waiting for the coffee machine to finish brewing, the colonel decided to pose a question to all assembled. He explained that his wife had been a bit frisky the night before and he failed to get his usual amount of sound sleep. He posed the question of just how much of sex was "work" and how much of it was "pleasure?

A Major chimed in with 75%-25% in favor of work. A Captain said it was 50%-50%. A Lieutenant responded with 25%-75% in favor of pleasure, depending upon his state of inebriation at the time.

There being no consensus, the colonel turned to the PFC who was in charge of making the coffee and asked for his opinion?

Without any hesitation, the young PFC responded, "Sir, it has to be 100% pleasure.

The colonel was surprised and as you might guess, asked why?

"Well, sir, if there was any work involved, the officers would have me and my fellow enlisted men doing it for them."

KGB

The phone rings at KGB headquarters. "Hello. What do you want?" "I'm calling to report my neighbor, Yankel as an enemy of the state. He is hiding undeclared diamonds in his firewood."

Next day, the KGB goons come over to Yankel's house. They search the shed where the firewood is kept, break every piece of wood, find no diamonds, swear at Yankel and leave.

The phone rings at Yankel's house. "Did the KGB come?" Yes." "Did they chop your firewood?" "Yes, they did." "Okay, now its your turn to call. I need my vegetable patch plowed."

Above all, believe—
in life, love, in yourself.

And if
there is
confusion on your field,
don't be afraid to call
time out and check in
with the Coach.

Dan Clark
AND ASSOCIATES

RELIGION

Observations

The Christians gave Him Sunday, the Jews gave Him Saturday, and the Muslims gave Him Friday. I guess it's only right that God has a three-day weekend!

I was thinking about how people seem to read the Bible a lot more as they get older, and then it dawned on me - they're cramming for their final exam!

Homeless Man

The preacher in an upscale eastside church was in the middle of his Sunday sermon when a homeless man walked in and sat down on a bench. Although his clothes were dirty, torn, and smelled of the streets, he carried a worn-out Bible in his hand.

As he sat down, the members of the congregation immediately slid away, held their noses, and scorned his presence.

When the preacher finished saving souls, he confronted the homeless man and said, "As you can see, this is a very posh, wealthy church and we have a dress code. So, if you ever decide to come back, you should pray and ask God what you should wear in a church like mine."

The homeless man left, only to return the very next Sunday in his same filthy, smelly clothes, carrying his worn-out Bible. As the members again scooted away from him on the bench in disgust, the preacher bee-lined it straight to the man and scolded him: "Didn't I tell you that before you came back you should pray to find out what the dress code is in a fancy church like this?"

The homeless man stood up straight and tall, looked the preacher square in the eyes, and replied, "Yes sir, I did ask God what I should wear in your church. But He told me He didn't know because He had never been here before!"

Moses

President Bush and his secret service are walking through a building when they see an old man with a beard and walking stick, wearing a robe and sandals. President Bush immediately sends over one of his men to speak to the man. "Excuse me, President Bush wants to know if you are Moses."

The old man lowers his head and doesn't say a word. Frustrated, President Bush walks over himself and asks, "Are you Moses?" This time, the old man turns his back and walks away. President Bush and his entourage storm off. Seeing what happened, a curious bystander approaches the old man and asks the same question, "Are you Moses?"

This time the old man answers, "Yes, I am. The bystander asks, "Then why didn't you acknowledge that to the president?" Moses answers, "Because the last time I talked to a bush, I ended up wandering in the wilderness for forty years and leading my people to the only place in the Middle East that doesn't have any Oil!"

Prayer

I asked God for a bike, but I know God doesn't work that way. So, I stole a bike and asked for forgiveness.

Become as a Little Child

A new Bishop was ordained in his church and the leaders asked his family to provide the devotional program during the service. When his youngest daughter stood at the pulpit she said, "This new calling for my dad has changed our entire family and what we are allowed to say around the house.

"It's been hard for us, but we no longer use the 'S' word and the 'F' word."

After two more family members spoke, the new Bishop

finally got the chance to talk. With a bright red face he said, "Just for the record, at our house the 'S' word is Shut up, and the 'F' word is Fart."

Life Lesson

A minister decided that a visual demonstration would add emphasis to his Sunday sermon. Four worms were placed into four separate jars.

The first worm was put into a container of alcohol. The second worm was put into a container of cigarette smoke. The third worm was put into a container of chocolate syrup. The fourth worm was put into a container of good clean soil. At the conclusion of the sermon, the Minister reported the following results:

Worm in the alcohol – Dead. Worm in the cigarette smoke – Dead. Worm in the chocolate syrup – Dead. Worm in the good clean soil – Alive.

The Minister then asked the congregation, "What did you learn from this demonstration?"

Maxine was sitting in the back, quickly raised her hand, and said, "As long as you drink, smoke and eat chocolate, you won't have worms!" (Which pretty much ended the service!

Faith

Two nuns were driving down a country road when they ran out of gas. They walked to a farmhouse, and a farmer gave them some gasoline, but the only container he had was an old bedpan. The nuns were happy to take whatever they were offered and returned to their car.

As they were pouring the gasoline from the bedpan into the tank of their car, a Protestant minister drove by. He stopped, rolled down his window, and said, "Excuse me, Sisters. I'm not of your religion, but I couldn't help admiring your faith!"

Adult Confession

A man went to confess his sins. In the confessional, he admitted that for years he had been stealing building supplies from the wood shop where he worked.

"What did you take?" the priest asked.

"Enough to build my house and three mountain cottages."

"This is very serious," the priest said. "I'll have to give you a stiff penance. Have you ever done a retreat?"

"No, Father, I haven't," the man replied. "But if you can get the plans, I can get the lumber!"

Teenage Confession

A teenage boy goes to church to confess his sins. "Forgive me Father for I have sinned with a loose girl." The priest asks, "Is that you Tommy O'Shaughnessy?" Tommy answers, "yes." The priest asks him who the girl is. Tommy replies, "I can't tell you Father. I don't want to ruin her reputation."

The priest asks, "Was it Lisa O'Connel? "No," answers Tommy. "Was it Cathy O'Callihan?" "No." "Was it Mary O'Malley?" "No." "Was it Fiona Slattery?" "No Father. I cannot tell you."

The priest says, "I admire you, but you have sinned and must atone. You can't be an Alter Boy for four months. You may go."

Tommy walks back to his pew and his friend Sean whispers, "What you'd get?" Tommy smiles and replies, "Four months of vacation and four good leads!"

Save Me

A man caught in a flood prayed to God for help. While he was on his knees praying, a police officer came to the door and offered to evacuate him, but he said, "No thanks, Officer, I'll stay here, God will deliver me," and resumed his prayers. Then a person in a rowboat came by as the waters were rising, and the man said, "No thanks, I'll stay here, God will deliver me" and continued praying to God for help.

The waters continued to rise and the man had to climb onto his roof. At last, a helicopter came with a ladder and the pilot told him to climb aboard. He again refused, all the while sitting on the roof and praying to God. Finally, the waters covered him and he drowned. After he got to heaven he told God how disappointed he was that God didn't answer his prayers.

God said, "What do you mean I didn't answer? I sent a police officer, a rowboat, and a helicopter; what else did you want?"

Medicine

Two doctors and an HMO manager die and line up together at the Pearly Gates. One doctor steps forward and tells St. Peter, "As a pediatric surgeon, I saved hundreds of children." St. Peter lets him enter.

The next doctor says, "As a psychiatrist, I helped thousands of people live better lives." St. Peter tells him to go ahead.

The last man says, "I was an HMO manager. I got countless families cost-effective health care."

St. Peter replies, "You may enter. But," he adds, "You

can only stay for three days. After that, you can go to hell."

Competence

A priest, a minister, and a rabbi want to see who's best at his job. So, they each go into the woods, find a bear, and attempt to convert it.

Later, they get together. The priest begins: "When I found the bear, I read to him from the Catechism and sprinkled him with holy water. Next week is his First Communion."

"I found a bear by the stream," says the minister, "and preached God's holy word. The bear was so mesmerized that he let me baptize him."

They both look down at the rabbi, who is lying on a gurney in a body cast. "Looking back," he says, "maybe I shouldn't have started with the circumcision."

Arrived

A man on holiday in Spain thought he would email his sister back in England. But he made a typo, so instead of sending it to Joan Foster, he sent it to Jean Foster, the wife of a recently deceased Protestant Pastor. She fainted when she read: "Arrived safely, but it sure is hot down here."

Where Is He

A couple had two little boys, aged eight and ten, who were excessively mischievous. The two were always getting into trouble and their parents could be confident that if any mischief occurred in their town, their two young sons were involved in some capacity.

At their wit's end as to what to do, the parents had heard that a clergyman in town had been successful in disciplining children in the past, so they contacted him, and he agreed to give it his best shot. He asked to see the boys individually, and the eight-year-old was sent to meet with him first. The clergyman sat the boy down and asked him sternly, "Where is God?"

The boy made no response, so the clergyman repeated the question in an even sterner tone, "Where is God?" Again, the boy made no attempt to answer, so the clergyman raised his voice even louder and screamed in the boy's face, "Where is God?"

At that, the boy bolted from the room, ran directly home, and slammed himself in his closet. His older brother followed him into the closet and asked, "What happened?" The younger brother replied, "We are in big trouble this time. God is missing and they think we are responsible!"

Religious Difference

A four-year-old Catholic boy was playing with a four-year-old Protestant girl in a backyard pool. When they took off their wet clothes, the little girl looked at the little boy and said, "Whoa, I didn't know there was that much difference between Catholics and Protestants."

Donations

After the church service, a little boy told the pastor, "When I grow up, I'm going to give you some money."

"Well, thank you," the pastor replied, "But why?"

"Because my daddy says you are one of the poorest preachers we've ever had."

Interpretation

A father was reading Bible stories to his young son. He read, "The man named Lot was warned to take his wife and flee out of the city, but his wife looked back and was turned to salt."

His son asked, "What happened to the flea?"

Heaven And Hell

Heaven is where the police are British, the chefs are Italian, the mechanics are German, the lovers are French, and everything is organized by the Swiss.

Hell is where the police are German, the chefs are British, the mechanics are French, the lovers are Swiss, and everything is organized by the Italians.

Mormons

There were three guys sitting behind three Mormons at a BYU versus University of Notre Dame football game. When BYU scored and went ahead in the game, the first one says to the others (loud enough for them to hear), "I think I want to move to New Jersey. I hear there are only a few hundred Mormons living there."

A few minutes later the second guy speaks up and says, "Yeah, I want to move to Boston. I hear there are only one hundred Mormons living there."

The third guy speaks up and says, "I want to move to Alaska. I hear there are only fifty Mormons living there."

Tired of their banter, one of the Mormons finally turned around, looked all three men in the eye and said, "I've got a better idea. Why don't all three of you guys go to hell - I hear there are no Mormons there!"

Punishment

A man was sent to hell for his sins. As he was being processed, he passed a room where a stockbroker he knew was having an intimate conversation with a beautiful woman.

"What a drag!" the man expressed. "I have to burn for all eternity and that stockbroker gets to spend it with that gorgeous woman."

The devil jabs the man with his pitchfork and yells, "Who are you to question that woman's punishment?"

The Preacher

A preacher was making his rounds on a bicycle to his parishioners when he came upon a little boy trying to sell a lawn mower.

"How much do you want for the lawn mower?" asked the preacher.

"I just want enough money to go out and buy me a bicycle," said the little boy.

The preacher asked, "Will you take my bike in trade for

it?"

"Mister, you've got yourself a deal."

The preacher took the mower and began to try to crank it. He pulled on the string a few times with no response. The preacher called the little boy over and said, "I can't get this mower to start."

The little boy said, "That's because you have to cuss at it to get it started."

The preacher said, "I am a minister, and I cannot cuss. It has been so long since I have been saved that I do not even remember how to cuss."

The little boy looked at him happily and said, "Just keep pulling on that string. It'll come back to ya!"

The Monastery

A guy joins a monastery and takes a vow of silence. He's allowed to say two words every seven years. After the first seven years, the elders bring him in and ask for his two words. "Cold floors," he says. They nod and send him away.

Seven more years pass. They bring him back in and ask for his two words. He clears his throat and says, "Bad food." They nod and send him away.

Seven more years pass. They bring him in for his two words. "I quit," he says.

"That's not surprising," the elders say. "You've done nothing but complain since you got here!"

The Priest

A priest was driving around observing conditions of the homes and yards of the members of his parish church. He came upon a situation where a member's car was parked in the driveway with two flat tires. It was leaking anti-freeze, and the windshield had been broken.

The priest also noticed the lawn had not been cut for some time, and the lawn mower was sitting there in need of repairs. The priest immediately went to the door to find out more about the existing problems. The member said he had lost his job, and then all these other things just seemed to develop one after another.

The priest said to the member, "This is the council I am going to give you to follow. Pick up your Bible with the back toward the table. Then drop it on the table and it will fall open. You are to then read the first two words you see and they will give you direction."

The member agreed and the priest left. A week later, the priest returned to see how things were going. He was amazed at what he saw. In the driveway was a new car, the lawn had been cut with the new riding mower, and all other things seemed to be in fine order. The priest went to the door and asked the member if he had followed all his instructions.

To which he replied, "Yes, Father, to the letter."

The priest then asked him, "What two words did you read when the Bible fell open?"

The member grinned and replied, "Chapter Eleven!"

An Atheist and a Bear

An atheist was walking through the woods, admiring all that the "accident of evolution" had created. "What majestic trees! What powerful rivers! What beautiful animals!" he said to himself.

As he was walking alongside the river he heard a rustling in the bushes behind him. As he turned to look, he saw a seven-foot grizzly bear charging toward him. He ran as fast as he could up the path. He looked over his shoulder and saw that the bear was closing in on him. Frantically he tried to run even faster, but he tripped and fell to the ground. He rolled over to pick himself up and saw the bear right beside him, raising its paw to kill him. At that instant he cried out, "Heaven have mercy!"

And time stopped. The bear froze. The forest was silent. The river even stopped flowing. A bright light shone upon the man, and a voice out of the sky said, "You deny my existence all these years, teach others that I don't exist, and even credit my creation to a cosmic accident, and now you expect me to help you out of this predicament? Am I to count you as a believer?"

The atheist, ever so proud, looked into the light and said, "It would be rather hypocritical to ask to be counted as a Christian after all these years, but could you make the bear a Christian?"

"Very well," said the voice.

And the light went out, the river flowed, the sounds of the forest continued, and the bear lowered its paw. The bear then brought both paws together, bowed its head, and said, "Lord, I thank you for this food which I am about to receive."

Convert For $10

Two old Jewish men are strolling down the street one day when they happen to walk by a Catholic church. They see a big sign posted that reads "Convert to Catholicism and Get $10." One of the men stops walking and stares at the sign. His friend turns to him and says, "Murray, what's going on?"

Murray replies, "I'm gonna do it," strides purposefully into the church and comes out about twenty minutes later with his head bowed.

"So," asks Abe, "did you get the ten dollars?"

Murray looks up at him and says, "Is that all you people think about?"

Jewish Rabbi

A Jewish father went to his Rabbi and exclaimed, "You won't believe what happened to me. My son left home and became a Christian. What do I do?" The Rabbi said, "You won't believe what happened to me. My son left home and became a Christian. I don't know what to do. Let's ask God. They prayed and Heavenly Father said, "You won't believe what happened to me!"

Church Bulletin Bloopers

Don't let worry kill you. Let the church help.

Due to the pastor's illness, Wednesday's healing service will be discontinued until further notice.

This being Easter Sunday, we will ask Mrs. Lewis to come forward and lay an egg on the altar.

Ladies Bible Study will be held at 10 a.m. All ladies are invited to lunch when the B.S. is done.

Low Self-Esteem Support Group will meet Thursday. Please use the back door.

At the evening service tonight, the sermon topic will be

"What is Hell?" Come early and listen to our choir practice.

You Won't Believe It

A Jewish father went to see his Rabbi and said, "Rabbi. You won't believe what happened to me. My son left home and became a Christian." The Rabbi said, "Whoa. You won't believe what happened to me. My son left home and became a Christian. What should we do?" They decided to pray and ask Heavenly Father. And Heavenly Father said, "You won't believe what happened to me!"

LOVIN' THE IRISH

The Blarney Stone

In the Village of Blarney,
There's one magic stone.
They say when you kiss it,
You're put in "the zone."
You talk and you gab.
And your words are so glib.
That it matters not least,
If it's truth or a fib.
So, it's lie through your teeth,
Or it's truth that you own.
It's all in the gift,
Of the kissed Blarney Stone.

Pulled Over

An Irish priest is driving along a country road when a policeman pulls him over. He immediately smells alcohol on the priest's breath and notices an empty wine bottle in the car.

He says, "Have you been drinking?"

"Just water," says the priest.

The cop replies: "Then why do I smell wine?"

The priest looks at the bottle and says, "Good Lord! He's done it again!"

An Irish Prayer

May those that love us, love us;
And those that don't love us,
May God turn their hearts.
And if He doesn't turn their hearts,
May He turn their ankles
So we'll know them by their limping.

Tequila Shots

Paddy goes into a bar and orders seven shots of tequila and one Guinness. The bartender lines up shots and goes to get the Guinness. When he comes back with the pint, all seven shots are gone. The bartender says, "Wow! You sure drank those fast."

Paddy explains: "You would drink fast too if you had what I have."

The bartender asks: "What do you have?"

The guy reaches into his pocket and says, "Fifty cents!"

Why Worry

There are only two things to worry about.

Either you are well or you are sick.

If you are well, then there is nothing to worry about.

But if you are sick, there are two things to worry about.

Either you will get well or you will die.

If you get well, there is nothing to worry about.

If you die, there are only two things to worry about.

Either you will go to heaven or hell.

If you go to heaven there is nothing to worry about.

But if you go to hell, you'll be so bloomin' busy shaking hands with friends you won't have time to worry!

Bank Robbery

A robber walks into an Irish bank and yells for everyone to stand in a line and turn around so they can't see him. He demands the money from the teller and because she saw his face he shot and killed her. The loud 'bang' startled a man at the front of the line who turned to see what was going on and the robber shot him too, yelling, "If anyone else looks at me I will kill them too." Just then Paddy steps out of line with one hand covering his eyes and the other hand raised in the air. Confused, the robber asked him what he wanted. With his eyes closed Paddy pointed at his wife standing next to him and exclaimed, "I haven't looked but I swear this woman just took a peek at you."

Cork

Billy stops Paddy in Dublin and asks for the quickest way to Cork.

Paddy says: "Are you on foot or in the car?"

Billy replies: "In the car."

"Well, that's the quickest way," says Paddy.

Dog

Gerry Connors walked his dog through the village every day. One day Mr. Connors is on his walk without the dog. His pal Billy sees him and asks, "Where is your dog?"

Mr. Murphy answers: "I had to have him put down."

"Was he mad?" asks Billy.

"He definitely wasn't too pleased," Murphy replies.

Toast

May your glass be ever full
With a roof over your head.
And may your soul rest an hour in heaven
Before the devil knows you're dead.

Last Request

A sobbing Mary Murphy approached Father O'Grady after mass. "What's bothering you?" he asked.

"Oh, Father, I've terrible news. My husband passed away last night."

The priest consoled her: "I'm so sorry. Did he have any last requests?"

"Certainly, Father," she replied. "He said, 'Mary put down the flippin gun...uuuugh!'"

Wild

His look is wild, his name is Fred

His red hair hides his Irish head
Take a peek, show no surprise
You cannot even see his eyes
Oh no, it must be as I feared
His mouth is covered by his beard
How does he breathe? How does he eat?
How does he see to cross the street?
Perhaps he can't see people stare
And cannot find the barber chair
Until he makes a barber stop
He will remain less man than mop

Car Park

An Irishman is struggling to find a parking space. "Lord," he prayed. "I can't stand this. If you open a space up for me, I swear I'll give up the Guinness and go to mass every Sunday." Suddenly, the clouds part and the sun shines on an empty parking spot. Without hesitation, the Irishman says: "Never mind, I found one!"

Sons

Two Irish mothers, Kate and Lorna were talking about their sons. Kate says, "My Patrick is such a saint. He works hard, doesn't smoke, and he hasn't so much as looked at a woman in over two years.'

Lorna responds, 'Well, my Francis is a saint himself. Not only has he not looked at a woman in over three years, but he hasn't touched a drop of liquor in all that time.'

"My word," says Kate, "You must be so proud."

"I am," announces Lorna, "and when he's paroled next month, I'm going to throw him a big party."

Fierce Dog

O'Connor was sitting in Ward's Irish bar with a large Rottweiler at his feet. "Does your dog bite?" asks Murphy. "No," replies O'Connor.

So, Murphy pats the dog who almost rips his arm off. "Hey," screams Murphy, 'You said your dog didn't bite!" Sheepishly O'Connor whispered, 'That's not my dog."

Grass

Michael O'Leary was waiting at the bus stop with his friend, Paddy Maguire, when a lorry flatbed truck went by loaded up with rolls of turf. "I'm gonna do that when I win de lottery, Maguire."

"What's that, Michael?" responds his mate.

"Send me lawn away to be cut," says O'Leary.

Heaven

When we drink, we get drunk.
When we get drunk, we fall asleep.
When we fall asleep, we commit no sin.
When we commit no sin, we go to heaven.
So, let's all get drunk, and go to heaven!

Obituary

Seamus opens the newspaper and is shocked to see his own obituary. In a panic, he phones his friend and asks: "Did you see the paper? They say I died!"

The friend replies: "Yes, I saw it! So, where ya calling from?"

Hazard Lights

Two County Kerry men were driving home one night when one asked the other to check if the car's Hazard Lights were working.

He promptly sticks his head out the window and says: "Yes, no, yes, no, yes, no."

Irish History

(If you lived in Ireland like I did for two years you would understand):

An Irishman, Englishman, and Scotsman are walking along the beach together when they trip over a lantern and a Genie pops out to grant each of them one wish.

The Scottish guy says, "I am a fisherman and want all the oceans full of fish."

The Genie blinks her eye and "poof" the oceans were swarming with fish.

The Englishman was amazed and said, "I want a wall around England, protecting her so that no one can ever get in."

Again, the Genie blinked and there was a huge wall around England.

The Irishman smiled and said, "Tell me about this wall."

The Genie explains, "It's 150 feet high, 50 feet thick, protecting England so that nothing can get in or out."

The Irishman says, "Fill it up with water."

Irish Limericks

There was a young fellow from Belfast,

That I wanted so badly to tell fast,

Not to climb up the stair,

As the top step was air,

And that's why the young fellow fell fast.

A wonderful bird is the pelican,

His bill holds more than his belican.

He can take in his beak,

Enough food for a week,

But I'm damned if I see how the helican.

Jokes Told Only In A Pub

Proud Father

A wealthy business owner in Waterford swaggered into a pub and started handing out cigars, proudly reporting that his wife had just given birth to a new baby boy! "How much did he weigh?" the bartender asked.

"Twenty-seven pounds," the father replied. And the waitress passed out!

One week later the same businessman walked into the

same pub filled with the same people and announced, "My son just lost nineteen pounds."

"How?" the concerned waitress asked.

Dad smiled, "Had him circumcised!"

Counseling

A Dublin psychiatrist was conducting a group therapy session with four young mothers and their young children. "You all have obsessions," he observed.

To the first mother he said, "You are obsessed with food, manifested by your daughter's name, Candy."

He turned to the second mother: "Your obsession is with money manifested by your daughter's name, Penny."

He turned to the third Mom, "Your obsession is alcohol, manifested by your daughter's name Brandy."

At this point, the fourth mother quickly got up, took her little boy by the hand, and whispered, "Come on, Dick, this guy has no idea what he's talking about. Let's go pick up your brother's Peter and Willy from school and get some dinner."

Farmer's Daughters

A farmer in rural County Leitrim had three beautiful triplet daughters whom he didn't allow to date until they turned twenty-one. Finally, that birthday arrived and the word that the three sisters were now eligible quickly spread throughout the countryside. Soon, the first gentleman caller knocked on the door. When farmer dad answered, the young man said, "Hi, my name is Joe, I'm here to take out your daughter Flo, and we're going to the show."

Dad said, "Okay, bring her home safe," and sent them on their way.

In a minute, a second gentleman caller knocked, Dad answered, and the young man said, "Hi, my name is Jay, I'm here to take out your daughter Fay, and we're going to the play."

Dad said, "Okay, bring her home safe," and sent them on their way.

Soon a third gentleman caller knocked. Dad answered. The young man said, "Hi, my name is Chuck." And he shot him!

Grill

One day in County Cork, a husband and wife are gardening when the husband rudely complains that her butt is as big as the grill. That night when they're lying in bed the husband asks for forgiveness and begs his wife to make love to him. The wife replied, "Do you really think I'm gonna fire up this big ass grill for one little weenie?"

Genie

Paddy was playing at Portmarnock Golf Club and made a hole-in-one. A genie popped out to grant him one wish. The man thought for a minute and said, "Make me 'Johnson larger."

"Done," said the genie and disappeared.

Continuing his game, the man noticed an immediate change in his "size." In two holes, it was down to his knee, and in two more holes it was dragging along the ground. 'This is horrible,' Paddy complained. 'I need another wish to fix this mess.' So, he concentrated and made another hole-in-one. Sure enough, the genie popped out and asked him what his new wish was.

Smiling, Paddy responded, "Make my legs longer!"

ON THE JOB / AT WORK

Reality?

Journalist: So how many employees are working at your company?

Business Owner: "Approximately half of them!"

Seriously?

When asked for his name by the coffee shop clerk, my friend answered, "Marc, with a C." Minutes later, he was handed his coffee with his name written on the side: Cark.

Competition

Mr. Ling owned a dry-cleaning store that had been in his family for three generations. Then a developer came along and wanted to push Mr. Ling out of his location.

Mr. Ling made it clear to the developer he was going to stay right where he was. To get even, the developer built the shopping mall around him and put cleaning shops on both sides of him to drive him out of business.

To combat the competition, Mr. Ling made a giant sign and hung it above his front door, which brought in more customers than he had ever had before. His sign said, "This Way To Main Entrance!"

No Competition

Rodney had opened his barbershop ten years ago and had always priced any cut at fifteen dollars. One day, a new shop opened up across the street, and in an attempt to steal his business, posted a sign advertising Six Dollar haircuts. Rodney immediately countered by hanging a new and bigger sign that read, "We Fix Six Dollar Haircuts!"

Clear Instructions?

The department store cashier told me 'Strip down, facing me.' How was I to know she meant my credit card!'

Cooking the Books?

An owner was interviewing for an accounting position. Each candidate was asked the same one question: How much is 1+1?

The first candidate replied, '2.' He left. The second candidate responded with the same answer, '2.' He left.

When the owner asked the third candidate he replied, 'How much do you want it to be?'

Career Opportunities

You see a gorgeous girl at a party. You go up to her and say, "I'm a fantastic lover." That's Direct Marketing.

You are at a party with a bunch of friends and see a gorgeous girl. One of your friends goes up to her and, pointing at you, says, "He's a fantastic lover." That's Advertising.

You see a gorgeous girl at a party. You go up to her and get her telephone number. The next day you call and say, "Hi, I'm a fantastic lover." That's Telemarketing.

You're at a party and see a gorgeous girl. You stand and straighten your tie, walk up to her, and pour her a drink. You open the door for her, pick up her bag after she drops it, offer her a ride, and then say, "I'm a fantastic lover." That's Public Relations.

You're at a party and see a gorgeous girl. She walks up to you and says, "I hear you're a fantastic lover." That's Brand Recognition.

Oh No

A doctor reaches into his smock to get a pen to write a prescription and pulls out a rectal thermometer. "Oh no," he proclaims, "So that's where I left my pen!"

Cunning

A dishonest crooked businessman and a senior citizen are sitting next to each other on a long flight. The businessman is thinking seniors are slow and he could take advantage of this elderly gentleman to make a few easy bucks before they land.

So, he asks if the senior would like to play a fun game. The senior is tired and just wants to take a nap, so he politely declines and tries to catch a few winks.

The ruthless businessman persists, saying that the game is a lot of fun — "I ask you a question, and if you don't know the answer, you pay me only $5.00. Then you ask me one, and if I don't know the answer, I will pay you $500.00," he says.

This catches the senior's attention and, to keep the businessman quiet, he agrees to play the game. The businessman asks the first question. "What's the distance from the Earth to the Moon?"

The senior doesn't say a word, but reaches into his pocket, pulls out a five-dollar bill, and hands it to the 'wheeler dealer.'

Now, it's the senior's turn. He asks the businessman, "What goes up a hill with three legs, and comes down with four?"

The lawyer uses his laptop to search all references he can find on the Net. He sends E-mails to all of the smart friends he knows; all to no avail. After an hour of searching, he finally gives up. He wakes the senior and hands him $500.00. The senior pockets the $500.00 and goes right back to sleep.

The crooked businessman is going nuts not knowing the answer, so he wakes the senior up and asks, "Well, so what goes up a hill with three legs and comes down with four?"

The senior reaches into his pocket, hands the lawyer $5.00, and goes back to sleep. Age and cunning will overcome youth, dishonesty and technology anytime.

Customer Service?

I love America and I'm not racist, but on your Customer Support Line why do you ask me to 'Press 1 for English,' and then put Bin Laden's sister on the phone?

My first computer — Delete / Print / Refresh

Starbucks

I'm baffled by what you need to know to order a drink at Starbucks. I swear I heard the woman in front of me say, 'I'll have a Grande, hot mocha, no foam, tri-soy hexagon vortex, shots of sugar-free vanilla, oat milk, hypothesis with filtered steamed ice to go with a sleave!'

Job Interview

Reaching the end of a job interview, the Human Resources Officer asks a young engineer fresh out of the Massachusetts Institute of Technology, "And what starting salary are you looking for?"

The engineer replies, "In the region of $125,000 a year, depending on the benefits package."

The interviewer inquires, "Well, what would you say to a package of five weeks' vacation, fourteen paid holidays, full medical and dental, company matching retirement fund to 50% of salary, and a company car leased every two years, say, a red Corvette?"

The engineer sits up straight and says, "Wow! Are you kidding?" The interviewer replies, "Yeah, but you started it."

Ya Gotta Love Attorneys

I sat next to a man on an airplane and asked him, what is your name? George. What do you do? I'm an attorney. How much do you charge? $5000 for four questions," the attorney replied. "Isn't that awfully high?" I asked. "Perhaps," the lawyer stated. "And what is your final question?"

Brilliant

A lawyer defending a man accused of burglary mounted an awesome creative defense:

"My client merely inserted his arm into the window and removed a few trifling articles. His arm is not himself, and I fail to see how you can punish the whole individual for an offense committed by his limb."

"Well put," the judge replied. "Using your logic, I sentence the defendant's arm to one year's imprisonment. He can accompany it or not, as he chooses."

The defendant smiled. With his lawyer's assistance, he detached his artificial limb, laid it on the bench, and walked out.

Defenseless

A defense attorney was cross-examining a police officer during a felony trial:

"Officer, did you see my client fleeing the scene?"

"No, sir, but a fellow officer provided the description of the offender running several blocks away."

"A fellow officer gave you the information. Do you trust your fellow officers?"

"Yes, sir, with my life." "With your life?" "Yes, sir."

"If you trust your fellow officers with your life, then why do you find it necessary to lock your locker in a room you share with those officers?"

"You see, sir, we share the building with a court complex, and sometimes defense attorneys have been known to walk through that room."

With that, the courtroom erupted in laughter, and a prompt recess was called.

Choking

A dad walks into a market with his young son. The father is holding a quarter in his teeth waiting to put it in a vending machine. Suddenly, the man starts choking, going blue in the face. The son realizes the father has swallowed the quarter and starts panicking, shouting for help.

A well dressed, attractive, but serious looking woman in a blue business suit is sitting at a coffee bar in the market reading her newspaper and sipping a cup of coffee. At the sound of the commotion, she looks up, puts her coffee cup down on the saucer, neatly folds her newspaper and places it on the counter. Then she gets up from her seat and makes her way, unhurriedly, across the market.

Reaching the man, the woman carefully but forcefully squeezes his neck, and then kicks him as hard as she can in the groin.

After a few seconds, the father convulses violently and coughs up the quarter, which the woman deftly catches in her free hand. Releasing the man, the woman hands the coin to the son and walks back to her seat in the coffee bar without saying a word.

As soon as he is sure that his father has suffered no lasting ill effects, the son rushes over to the woman and starts thanking her profusely, saying, "I've never seen anybody do anything like that before. It was fantastic. Obviously, you've had a lot of practice doing that. Are you a doctor?"

"No," she says, "I'm a divorce attorney."

Fair Judge

A judge enters the courtroom and starts the proceedings, saying: "Before this process starts in earnest, there is one thing I have to clear first. The plaintiff gave me $10,000 so I would rule in his favor.

The defendant gave me $12,000 so I would rule in her favor. To make this case a fair one, I'm hereby returning $2,000 to the defendant."

The Raise

Sam walks into his boss's office and says, "Sir, I'll be straight with you, I know the economy isn't great, but I have over three companies after me, and I would like to respectfully ask for a raise."

After a few minutes of haggling, the boss finally agrees to a 5% raise, and Sam happily gets up to leave. "By the way," asks the boss, "Which three companies are after you?"

"The electric company, water company, and phone company!"

Hot Shot

A young businessman had just started his own firm. He rented a beautiful office and had it furnished with antiques. Sitting there, he saw a man come into the outer office. Hoping to look like a hotshot, the businessman picked up the phone and started to pretend he was working on a big, important business deal.

He threw huge figures around and made giant commitments. Finally, he hung up and asked the visitor, "Can I help you?"

The man said, "Yeah, I've come to activate your phone lines."

Day Off

An employee goes to see his supervisor in the front office.

"Boss," he says, "We're doing some heavy house cleaning at home tomorrow, and my wife needs me to help with the attic and the garage, moving and hauling stuff."

"We are shorthanded," the boss replies. "I can't give you the day off."

"Thanks, boss," says the employee, "I knew I could count on you!"

Order of Operations

The sales chief, the HR chief, and the boss of a company are on their way to lunch when they stumble upon a beat-up, but valuable looking brass container.

The sales chief picks it up and starts cleaning it with his

handkerchief. Suddenly, a genie emerges out of a curtain of purple smoke. The genie is grateful to be set free and offers them each a wish.

The HR chief is wide-eyed and ecstatic. She says, "I want to be living on a beautiful beach in Jamaica with a sailboat and enough money to make me happy for the rest of my life."

Poof! She disappears.

The sales chief says, "I want to be happily married to a wealthy supermodel with penthouses in New York, Paris, and Hong Kong."

Presto! He vanishes.

"And how about you?" asks the Genie, looking at the boss. The boss scowls and says, "I want both of those idiots back in the office by 2 PM."

Moral: Always let your boss speak first!

The Paper Shredder

A young executive is leaving the office late one evening when he finds the CEO standing in front of a shredder with a piece of paper in his hand.

"Listen," said the CEO, "This is a very sensitive and important document here, and my secretary has gone for the night. Can you make this thing work for me?"

"Certainly," the young executive says. He turns the machine on, inserts the paper, and presses the start button.

"Excellent, excellent!" says the CEO as his paper disappears inside the machine. "I just need one copy."

Sales Champ (In Memory of 'Doc' Sansom)

Three guys begin work at a toothbrush company as salesmen. Each day, two of the guys sell 20 toothbrushes each, and the third guy consistently sells 200. The other two guys are jealous, but they can't figure out his secret. Then, one day, they run into him at the mall, where he's set up a table to sample potato chip dip.

"This is your secret?" says the first guy.

"Yep. Try some dip," says the third. They both take a chip and super-scoop some dip.

"Ech!" gasps the second guy. "This tastes like dog poop!"

"It is dog poop! Would you like to buy a toothbrush?"

Microscope

Store Clerk: "Can I interest you in a microscope?"

Customer: "No thanks. I have no use for it."

Clerk: "Here is my business card in case you ever do."

Customer: "I can't read this. It's too small."

Clerk: "Boy, have I got a solution for you!"

My Dad's Two Favorite Jokes that Always Made Him Laugh. (In tribute to my amazing father whom I never heard swear or lie, these are his all-time favorite examples of tell-it-like-it-is, to-the-point communication):

Rover

I'd been trying to take out Millie Lou for a long time. Finally, she said yes. She wanted to take me to her favorite restaurant. Wouldn't you know it - she loves chili. I was a bit nervous because I knew what chili did to me, but I was starving, so I tanked it down and ate a lot more than I should have.

At the end of the evening, Millie Lou wanted me to meet her family. We went to her house and gathered in the family room. Her dad, mom, brother, sister, me, Millie Lou, even the dog was there sitting by my feet. Let's face it. I'm only human, and as the conversation progressed, the chili started to get to me. So, I let a little gas out. Millie Lou's dad said, "Rover."

I thought, Great, he thinks it's the dog. So, I let a little more out.

Again, Millie Lou's dad said, "Rover."

I thought, Perfect, he knows it's the dog. So, I let it all out. Just then Millie Lou's dad stands up and yells, "Rover, get over here boy before he shits on you!"

Fastest Gun

An outlaw cowboy decides he wants to become the fastest gun in the west. So, he buys two six-guns and practices every day for a year. When he finds Billy the Kidd in a wild-west saloon, he walks up to him and proclaims, "I am the fastest gun in the west." Billy the Kidd says, "Prove it."

The guy looks around the saloon and says, "See the three buttons on the left sleeve of the piano player? Count 'em."

Billy the Kidd counts "one, two," but before he gets to three, the guy draws with his left pistol and shoots off all the buttons on the piano players left sleeve. The cowboy continues, "See the three buttons on the right sleeve of the piano player? Count 'em."

Billy the Kidd counts one, two, but before he gets to three the guy draws with his right pistol and shoots off the three buttons on the right sleeve of the piano player.

Boastfully he asked, "So what do you think?"

Billy the Kidd smiled and said, "If I was you, I'd go out

behind the saloon and find the big tub of lard by the door. Then I'd dip both of your guns in it until they are completely coated and lubricated."

Defiantly, the cowboy asked, "Why should I do a stupid thing like that?" Billy the Kidd smirked, "Because when Wyatt Earp gets through playing the piano he's gonna cram both of them right up your ass!"

Over Worked

For a couple of years, I've been blaming it on lack of sleep and too much pressure from my job, but now I found out the real reason: I'm tired because I'm overworked.

As of 2019, the population of America is 337 million, of which 204 million are retired. That leaves 133 million to do the work.

There are 85 million in school, which leaves 48 million to do the work.

Of this, there are 29 million employed by the federal government, plus 2.8 million in the Armed Forces, which leaves 16.2 million to do the work.

Take from the total the 14.8 million people who work for state governments and that leaves 1.4 million to do the work.

At any given time, there are 188,000 people in

hospitals, leaving 1,212,000 to do the work.

Now, there are 1,211,988 people in prisons. That leaves just two people to do the work - you and me. And you're sitting here with this joke book!

OTHER BOOKS AVAILABLE BY
DAN CLARK

The Art of Significance-Achieving the Level Beyond Success
(Audiobook Also Available)

The Art of Significance Study Guide
Training Manual

The Art of Significant Relationships
(15 Author Anthology)

The Art of Raising Significant Children

Influential Impact
The Art of Significant Leadership

Speak Like a Pro
The Art of Significant Speaking and Storytelling

Transference of Trust
The Art of Significant Selling

Story Selling

Making of a Champion
The Art of Significant Team Building

The Art of Significant Network Marketing
(Audiobook and Study Guide)

Chicken Soup for the College Soul

The Most Popular Stories by Dan Clark in
Chicken Soup for the Soul

Puppies for Sale
(Illustrated Children's Storybook)

Soul Food
(The Complete Dan Clark Collection)

Puppies for Sale
and Other Inspirational Tales

The Treasury of Dan Clark Quotes,
Lyrics and Poems

CONTACT DAN AT:

Website: danclark.com

Email: info@danclark.com

Office: 800-676-1121

www.ingramcontent.com/pod-product-compliance
Lightning Source LLC
Chambersburg PA
CBHW031924190326
41519CB00007B/400